T0246244

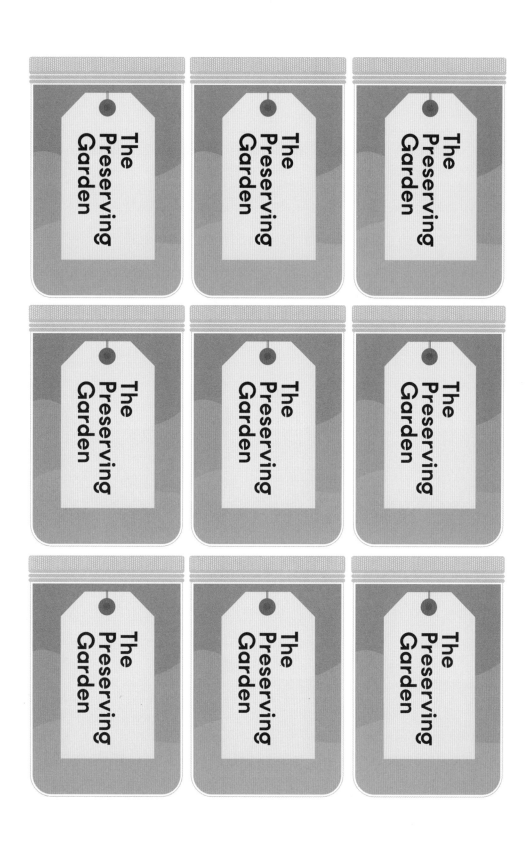

For Mum, my first preserving and cooking teacher.
And for Marni, because almost fifty years of friendship feels
like a blessing and a wonder that should not go unremarked.

The Preserving Garden

Jo Turner

Bottle, pickle, ferment and cook homegrown food all year round

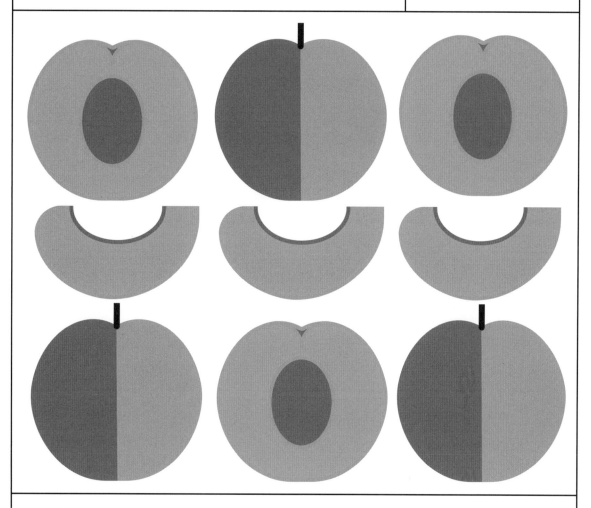

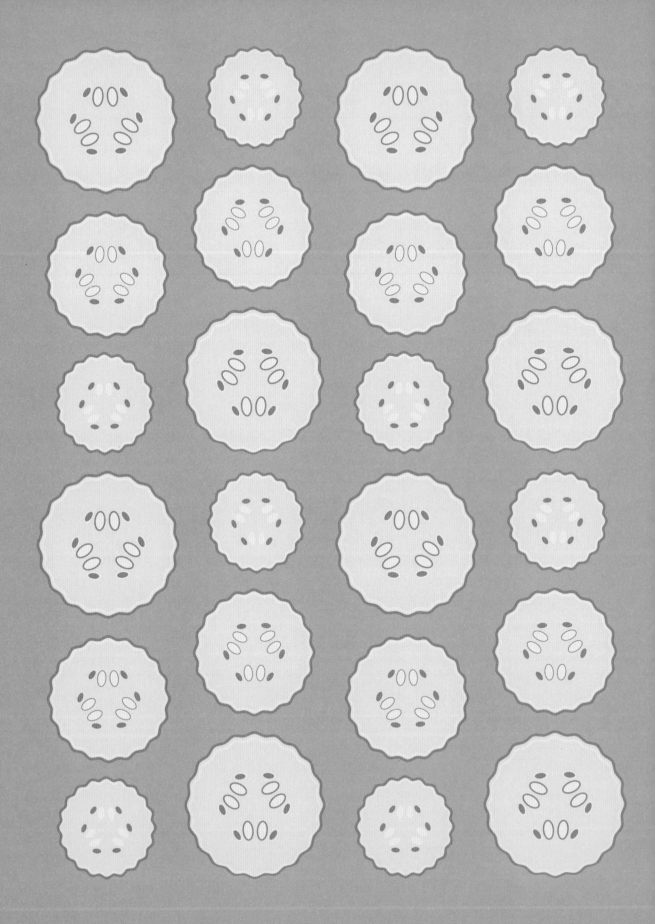

Contents

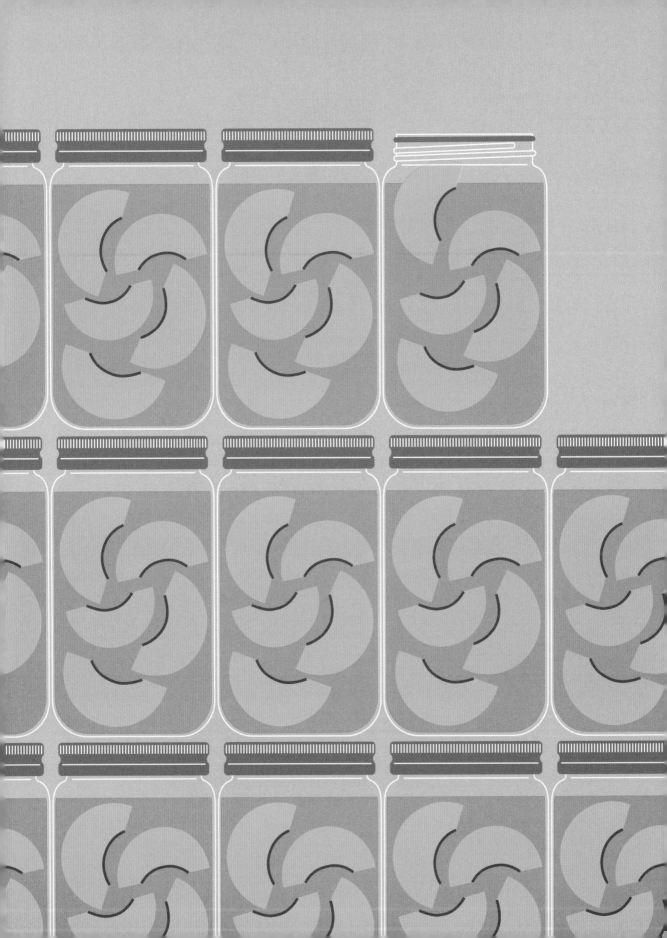

Introduction

With all my senses, I can recall sitting at the table in my nan's kitchen with my mum and aunt as they worked to transform a wooden crate of yellow peaches into jars and jars of bottled fruit – sunny orbs ready to enjoy over the coming twelve months. The day began with a trip to the train station to collect the peaches sent from a cousin's orchard. We took them home to my nan's blue house and sat in the cool of her kitchen, the drawn blind muting the intense summer light. As I cast my mind back, I can hear my nan's croaky voice, smell the sweet peaches, and see her hands work deftly to peel, pit and slice. I can hear the squeak and thwack as rubber rings are expertly slipped around the tops of jars to be packed tightly with fruit, filled with syrup and clipped shut. It was a production line and a family ritual and, I am sure, where my love of preserving began. Making something from an abundance feels like good work, practical and creative. There is enormous satisfaction in hands-on involvement, from planting to preserving. Using fruit or vegetables grown in your own yard reduces food miles, waste and plastic use, and gives you control over what goes into the food you eat – all very contemporary concerns addressed by an old-fashioned practice.

We were lucky; having family with large orchards meant we had access to an abundance of seasonal fruit. Growing and preserving food doesn't need to be a factory-size operation. One or two jars of raspberry and redcurrant jelly, made with fruit picked in summer, is a cheery balm in the grey depths of winter. Most of the recipes in this book can be scaled up to make use of a larger crop. Of course, as you wait for fruit trees to become productive, you can take advantage of seasonal availability at farmers' markets. This will give you the time to practise your preserving techniques; identifying and developing your favourite ways to get the most out of every season.

You can plan a preserving garden by choosing varieties for specific end-uses, planting the fruits and vegetables you use or crave the most. Or you can take a laissez-faire approach – planting what takes your fancy and discovering ways to preserve the fruit and vegetables harvested. I tend to do a little of both, putting my 'must have' crops at the top of the list and introducing something new each season.

Planting a fruit garden is truly an exercise in investment gardening; fruit and nut trees take time to produce a crop, but will continue to do so for years to come. Alternatively, a veggie patch is the fastest path to preserving homegrown produce. Make sure to choose a variety of reliable annuals, including herbs, that lend themselves to multiple uses in the preserving kitchen. Not only does a preserving garden supply the freshest seasonal produce for you to harvest and use beyond their growing seasons, but it also allows you to grow hard-to-source plants, and select species and varieties that best suit your intended use: tomatoes for sauces, autumn-cropping pears for spiced chutney, and sweet and sour cherries for bottling and drying.

I can't say what gives me more satisfaction and joy: the sight of a thriving garden heavy with fruit and vegetables, or pantry shelves lined with bottles and jars of preserves. From planting to preserving, I hope this book encourages you to make the most out of your homegrown produce all year round.

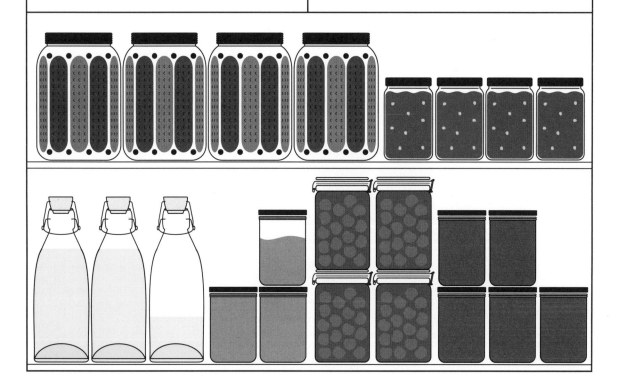

Chapter 01

How to preserve

Types of preserves

Bottled fruit

There are times when you have an abundance of fruit and little inclination or inspiration to turn it into something else. When these occasions arise, the fastest and most satisfying response is to 'bottle' whole, halved or sliced fruit in water or syrup. If you are in Australia and own a Fowlers preserving kit, this can be done by packing jars and processing for 1 hour, no matter the size of the jar or quantity or variety of fruit. If you don't have a preserving kit, using the water bath method is an efficient and accessible process (see page 14). If you want to experiment and add flavours to bottled fruits, refer to the preserving charts from page 195 for suggested companions.

Chutney and relish

Chutney and relish both mix fruit or vegetables with spices and herbs. Relish usually contains vegetables and has a pronounced vinegary flavour, while chutney is thicker and sweeter and typically contains fruit cooked until very soft: I think of it as a rich, savoury jam.

Jam, jelly and marmalade

To make jam, fruit and sugar are cooked together until the fruit breaks down and pectin is released to dissolve in the juices. The method for marmalade is similar, with some recipes calling for the additional step of soaking finely sliced peel before cooking. For jelly, the cooked fruit mixture is strained through muslin, and the resulting liquid is cooked with sugar (around 450 g/1 lb to every 600 ml/1¼ pints of liquid) until a set is achieved. Too much sugar will make a soft, syrupy jelly; too little and the result will be rubbery.

Use plain white sugar for fruit jams and jellies as it does not alter the colour or flavour of the fruit. Feel free to experiment with different types of sugar but avoid artificial sweeteners; they do not provide the setting power of sugar and can impart a bitter flavour when cooked.

To test if jam, jelly or marmalade has reached setting point, place a small saucer in the freezer as you put the fruit on to cook. When you think it's nearly ready, turn off the heat and place a teaspoon of the preserve mixture on the chilled saucer. Return to the freezer, and after a few minutes gently push it with your finger; the surface should pucker or wrinkle. Don't fret if your first test is unsuccessful – simply return the saucer to the freezer and the pan to the heat for another 5 minutes, then test again.

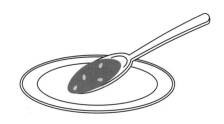

A note on pectin

Pectin is a naturally occurring fibre that, when combined with sugar and acid, forms a bond that causes jam to set. All fruits have different levels of pectin; strawberries are notoriously low in this setting agent, while crabapples have very high levels and are often cooked with other fruits for this reason.

I have included a note about the pectin levels found in each variety of fruit. They are at their highest when fruit is unripe, so choose just-ripe or slightly under-ripe fruit to make jam and jelly. The peel, pips, juice and pith of citrus fruit can improve the setting qualities of fruits with moderate pectin levels. Tie the peel, pips and pith in a small muslin bag and add to the preserving pan. Liquid and powdered pectin are colourless, flavourless extracts made from high-pectin fruits and can be used to set jam and jelly made with low-pectin fruit.

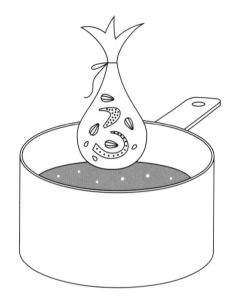

Pickling and fermenting

Both pickling and fermenting create a delicious sour flavour; the difference between the two is how that is achieved. Pickled foods rely on an acidic brine containing salt and vinegar, while fermented foods utilise naturally occurring sugars and bacteria to create a chemical reaction.

The acidity level is crucial to the safety, flavour and texture of pickled vegetables, and changing the ratio of vinegar, water and vegetables can affect all of these qualities. The vinegar must have an acid content of at least 5 per cent, so check the label before use; apple cider vinegar and rice vinegar, for example, do not always have the required level of acidity.

Use un-iodised salt as it produces a clear pickling liquid. The same goes for white sugar; brown sugar may be used but it will affect the colour and clarity.

For the flavourings, use whole spices and washed fresh herbs as they give the best flavour and appearance. Dried herbs and ground spices will make the brine cloudy.

Select firm young vegetables free of blemishes and use within 24 hours of picking. (Purchased fruit and vegetables should be sourced from a reliable supplier and used as soon as humanly possible – certainly no later than 24 hours after purchase.) Wash and drain all produce before use.

Metal lids are not suitable for sealing jars with vinegary contents. Look for lids that have a non-metallic barrier or film on the underside.

Many brined vegetables can be stored in the fridge for 2–3 weeks. Processing in a water bath extends the shelf-life considerably.

Preserving methods

Straight-sided bottles of cherries, peaches and apricots come to mind when I think about preserving. I can still see the big, green metal urn my nan used to process jars of fruit – a mysterious stovetop beast that was ungainly and mildly terrifying. Thankfully, it is now possible to purchase a preserving kit that is lightweight, electric and easy to use. Jars are packed with fruit or vegetables, filled with liquid, and then sealed and heated. It couldn't be easier, and I still use this method for processing large quantities of seasonal fruit. That said, you don't need a preserving kit to make the recipes in this book – in fact, they are written with smaller batches in mind, suitable for processing in a large saucepan or stockpot.

Water bath information

Processing times vary, depending on the method used to fill jars. A **raw pack** uses uncooked food and a hot liquid. A **hot pack** heats fruits and vegetables before placing them in jars and then covering them with a hot liquid. **Headspace** refers to the unfilled space between the jarred contents and the lid. This space is essential for all preserves that are processed in a water bath as it allows for the expansion of contents during processing and the formation of a vacuum seal as the jars cool. The required headspace is stated in each recipe.

It is important to note that not all produce is safe to process in a water bath. Typically, vegetables that grow under or close to the ground should not be treated with this method. The safest approach is to stick to fruits, and preserve anything not listed in the chart (on page 194) by following a recipe.

Specific preserving times in a boiling water bath depends both on what is being processed (see Food safety opposite) and the size of the jar or bottle. This information is included in each recipe. For this method you will need the following equipment:

- a large stockpot with a lid and the capacity to fully submerge jars by 3 cm (1¼ inches)
- a rack or folded tea towel to sit in the bottom of the pan

- jars and lids
- a pair of preserving tongs to lift the jars in and out of hot water.

Place a rack or folded tea towel in the bottom of the pan, add the sealed jars and fill with enough water to cover the jars by 3 cm (1¼ inches). Cover with the lid and bring to the boil. The processing time begins when the water has come to a rapid boil. The water must boil for the entire processing time; if the temperature drops, bring it back to a rapid boil and restart the timing from the beginning.

At the end of the processing time, turn off the heat, remove the lid from the pan and allow the jars to sit for 5 minutes. Carefully remove them with preserving tongs and place on a tea towel, then leave at room temperature for 12–24 hours. To check whether the jars have sealed properly, press down on the centre of the lids – they should not spring back when you lift your finger (you may have heard the satisfying 'pop' of jars sealing as they sat cooling on the bench). Tapping the lid of a sealed jar with a teaspoon will produce a high-pitched ringing sound; a dull sound indicates no seal or food in contact with the lid. But don't despair: jars of preserves that have failed to seal can be stored in the fridge and consumed within 7 days.

Please note that altitude can affect the time it takes for water to boil, and therefore the time needed to process safely in a water bath.

Food safety

Safe preserving depends on removing oxygen, destroying enzymes, preventing the growth of bacteria, yeast and mould, and creating a tight vacuum seal. Botulism spores exists on the surface of most foods, and because they only grow in the absence of air, they are harmless on fresh food. However, moist, low-acid foods, temperatures between 4°C (40°F) and 50°C (122°F) and oxygen levels below 2 per cent promote the development of the deadly botulism toxin. The correct processing time, sterilised and tightly sealed bottles, and proper acid levels mitigate against preserved food spoiling. Preserved foods should be stored at temperatures between 10°C (50°F) and 20°C (68°F) and refrigerated after opening.

Damaged produce can harbour microorganisms that will spoil food, so try to use unblemished fruit and vegetables if possible; if there is evidence of insect damage or bruising just cut away the affected areas. Make sure the produce is well washed before you begin.

Low-acid foods, such as tomatoes and figs, need additional acid in the form of vinegar, fresh lemon juice or citric acid before they can be safely processed in a water bath.

The instructions in the recipes should produce safe, shelf-stable preserves; however, if you see mould or bubbles, detect a strange odour, hear a fizz or have any doubts about your preserve's quality or safety, throw it away. Always store opened preserves in the fridge.

Sterilising and filling jars

Impeccably clean jars, lids and sealing rings are essential for safe, long-lasting preserving. Only use jars that are free of flaws; discard any with cracks, nicks or uneven edges. Lids should be unblemished with smooth rims to ensure a clean seal with the jar. Metal lids should not be used to seal jars or bottles containing brined or pickled produce – use glass or metal lids sealed with a plastic-like coating on the underside.

To sterilise before use, wash the jars, lids and rings (if using) in hot soapy water, then rinse them in a sink of clean hot water. Leave the lids to air-dry on a clean tea towel. Place the rings in a bowl of water; they should be wet when jars are sealed. Stand still-damp jars upside down on a baking tray lined with an old, clean tea towel and place in a warm (170°C/325°F) oven for 15–20 minutes. Turn the oven off and leave the jars to keep warm until needed. Jars should be filled while they are still warm so they don't crack when filled with hot contents or placed in a boiling water bath.

A wide-mouthed preserving funnel is a life-changing piece of equipment. Not only does it allow you to fill jars quickly, it helps to keep the rims clean. The easiest way to fill jars is to place the pan of preserves in the sink and stand the jars on the draining board lined with a tea towel. Then use a small jug to funnel jam into each jar. To ensure a proper seal, wipe the rims with a clean, damp cloth or paper towel before sealing with the lids.

Jars of jam, jelly, relish and chutney not processed in a water bath should be allowed to cool completely before sealing to avoid condensation forming and spoiling the contents.

A note on jars, bottles and pans

While scrupulously sterilised jars and bottles, processing times and some ingredient ratios are critical to successful preserving, there is a degree of flexibility when it comes to container size.

The recipes offer a guide to make the process practical and accessible, but these may be adapted to suit the quantities you are preserving.

Always choose a heavy-based pan large enough to fit all the ingredients comfortably. You want to be able to stir the mixture without fear of being splashed by lava-like eruptions of the boiling, sugar-heavy contents.

Spoon and cup measures

This book uses 20 ml (4 teaspoon) tablespoon measures. If you are using a 15 ml (3 teaspoon) tablespoon measure, please add an extra teaspoon for each tablespoon specified.

We also use 250 ml cup measures. US cups are 240 ml so please adjust accordingly.

LIQUID VOLUME

ML/LITRES	FL OZ	CUPS
30 ml	1 fl oz	
60 ml	2 fl oz	¼ cup
80 ml	2½ fl oz	⅓ cup
100 ml	3½ fl oz	
125 ml	4 fl oz	½ cup
160 ml	5½ fl oz	⅔ cup
180 ml	6 fl oz	¾ cup
200 ml	7 fl oz	
250 ml	8½ fl oz	1 cup
300 ml	10 fl oz	
350 ml	12 fl oz	
400 ml	13½ fl oz	
500 ml	1 pint	2 cups
1 litre	1 quart	4 cups

Peeling fruit

Remove skin from peaches and tomatoes by making a small cross at the base with a sharp knife. Soak in boiling water for 30–60 seconds, then refresh in cold water to stop the fruit from becoming mushy. The skins should easily lift away from the flesh.

Syrups

Instructions for bottling fruit often reference a light, medium or heavy syrup. The quantities below are a good starting point but can always be adjusted according to personal taste.

LIGHT SYRUP

150 g (5½ oz) sugar

1.5 litres (1½ quarts) water

MEDIUM SYRUP

300 g (10½ oz) sugar

1.5 litres (1½ quarts) water

HEAVY SYRUP

650 g (1 lb 7 oz) sugar

1.5 litres (1½ quarts) water

Place the sugar and water in a saucepan and stir over medium heat until the sugar has dissolved. Bring to the boil, then pour over the fruit in the jars.

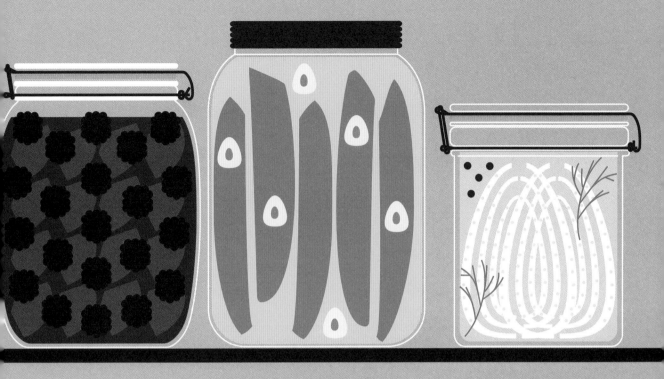
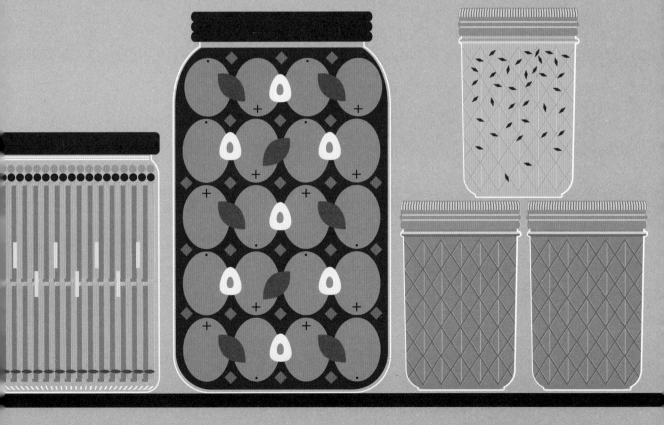

Chapter 02

Preserved vegetables

How and where you plant a vegetable garden depends on the available space and time, and ultimately what you aim to achieve. If you have a large plot, and lots of time and energy, dream big and plan a series of beds planted with a rotation of crops. If the space available is a sunny balcony, it is still possible to grow fruits and vegetables to preserve. Don't forget to think vertically – existing walls and fences can support climbing plants such as beans, passionfruit and cucumbers. No matter the situation, the basics of starting and maintaining a vegetable garden are the same. Varying degrees of sun, water and food are almost all that plants need to thrive. Or perhaps you want to grow something you can't find at the greengrocer or that has a very short season. The most straightforward approach is to buy and plant seedlings. As your understanding of what grows best in your garden, and any preference for particular preserves develops, you may be inspired to seek specific varieties of fruits and vegetables. Creating, tending and harvesting a garden can easily become an obsession; with planting schemes to be plotted, varieties to be discovered and trialled, and new recipes to be tweaked and developed. Watching as a tiny seed or seedling becomes a thriving plant and a source of food is as rewarding as it is reassuring.

Cucumber

Cucumis sativus

One or two climbing cucumbers will produce a good supply of summer and autumn fruit, with more than enough to make jars of gherkins and Bread and butter pickles (see page 26, swap zucchini for an equal quantity of cucumber). Cucumbers that will be used to make gherkins should be picked when small. Because they grow on a frame or support, these plants are great space-savers.

♈	**Plant** spring, summer
◎	**Harvest** summer, autumn
❦❦	**Needs cross-pollination** no
⊽	**Pot** yes, compact varieties
☼	**Aspect** full sun
✳	**Frost tolerant** no
⇩	**Soil pH** 6.6–7.5

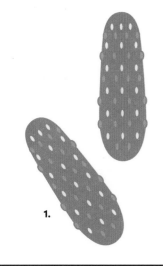

1.

Cucumber

1. Parisian Pickling (picked young)
2. National Pickler
3. Parisian Pickling

Varieties
Parisian Pickling – picked young to make cornichons or left to grow for gherkins
National Pickler – deep green with dark stripes, pick when they reach 5–10 cm (2–4 inches) in length to make gherkins

Nurture
Choose a sunny, well-drained position and dig in rotted manure and compost. Form a row of mounds to which you have added more manure or compost and plant two or three seeds in the top of each mound. Thin seedlings to 40–50 cm (16–20 inches) between plants. Most varieties will need staking or support, and stakes should be placed when planting the seeds. When seedlings have five to six leaves, pinch out the growing tips to encourage side shoots. Keep plants well watered and feed with liquid fertiliser every 4–6 weeks during the growing period and every 2 weeks when fruit is forming. Cucumbers can be grown in a pot that is at least 1 m (3 feet) deep and has good drainage. Look for a compact variety and place a frame in the pot when planting seeds. To pollinate flowers by hand, remove the petals from a male flower (they grow in clusters of three to five and have shorter stems) to expose the pollen-covered stamen. Carefully insert the exposed stamen into a female flower (they grow individually on longer stems and will have a small fruit at their base) to transfer the pollen to the female flower's stigma.

Flavour companions
chives, coriander, cumin, dill, garlic, lemon, mint, olive, paprika, parsley, spring onion, strawberry, tomato

Ways to preserve
pickled

How to use
salads, sandwiches, burgers, sauce ravigote, potato salads

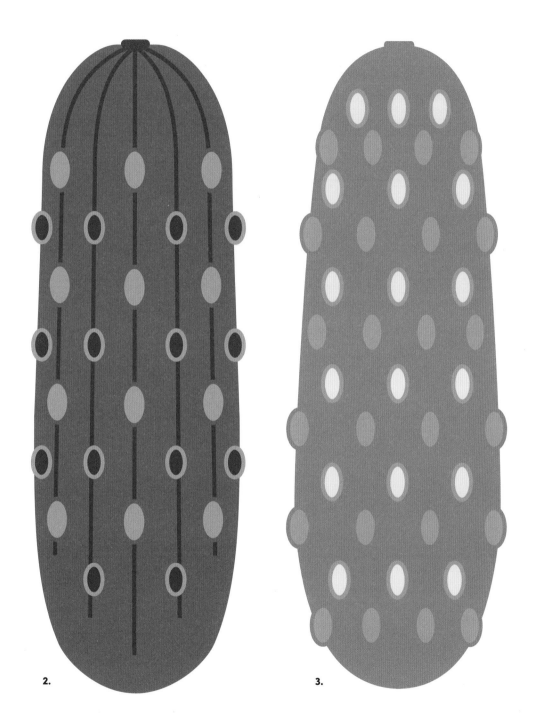

2.

3.

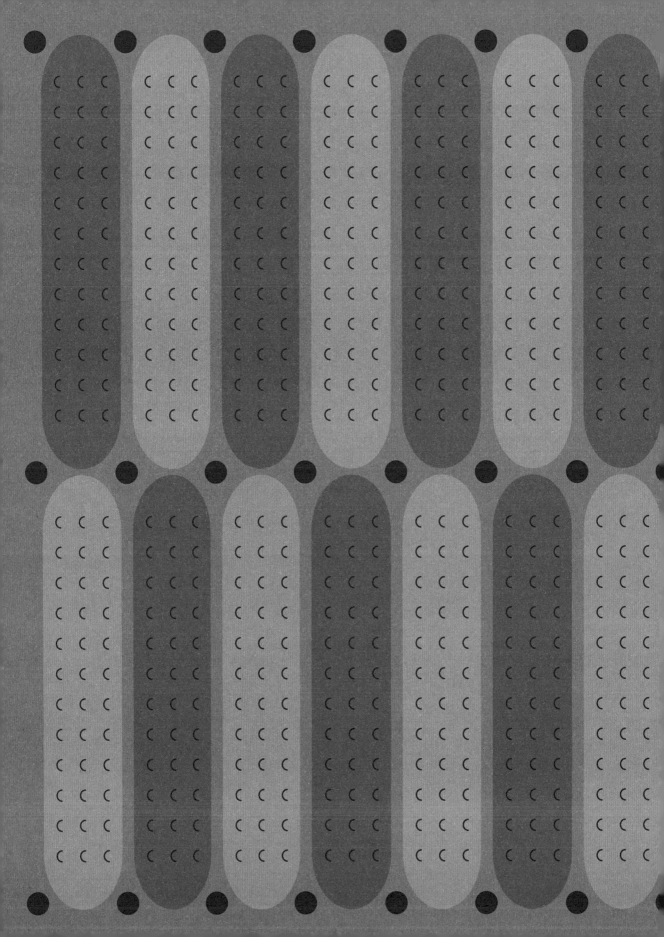

Gherkins

I love the crunch and sweet, sharp flavour of these gherkins. They're great on their own but also provide a pleasing contrast when finely diced and added to potato salads.

....

To make the pickling spice, combine all the ingredients, then store in a jar until needed. This makes more than you will need for this recipe, but it keeps well in an airtight jar for up to 3 months.

Place the cucumbers in a non-reactive bowl, sprinkle with the salt and leave to soak for 3–4 hours. Shortly before this time is up, bring the vinegar and 250 ml (1 cup) water to the boil.

Tip the cucumbers into a colander and pour over some boiling water. Drain and rinse again, then pack into two warm sterilised 250 ml (8½ fl oz) jars (see page 15). Add a dill sprig (or a small pinch of fennel seeds) and 1 teaspoon pickling spice to each jar, along with any additional flavourings. Pour in the hot vinegar mixture, leaving 1 cm (½ inch) headspace.

Remove any air bubbles by gently running a small spatula down and around the side of the jars. Wipe the rims, seal the jars and process in a water bath for 15 minutes (see page 14). Leave the gherkins in a cool, dark place for 4 weeks before using, then refrigerate after opening.

500 g (1 lb 2 oz) cucumbers (picked when small), washed and dried

35 g (1¼ oz) fine salt

250 ml (1 cup) white vinegar

boiling water, to rinse

2 dill sprigs (or 2 small pinches of fennel seeds)

optional flavourings (peeled garlic cloves, whole black peppercorns and/or small tarragon sprigs)

Pickling spice

2 tablespoons yellow mustard seeds

1 tablespoon whole allspice

2 teaspoons coriander seeds

1 teaspoon chilli flakes

1 teaspoon ground ginger

6 whole cloves

2 bay leaves, crumbled

1 cinnamon stick

2 x 250 ml (8½ fl oz) sterilised jars

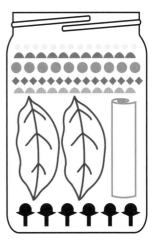

Zucchini

1. Black Coral
2. Golden Zebra
3. Costata Romanesco

1.

Zucchini (courgette)

Cucurbita pepo

Zucchini are a relatively easy-to-grow vegetable, and it is quite common for one or two plants to get away from you, with very large and not very flavoursome fruit hiding under large leaves. Zucchini should be picked small and often, take the time to lift leaves and search for hidden fruit.

Plant spring, summer

Harvest summer, autumn

Needs cross-pollination can be hand pollinated

Pot yes

Aspect sunny, open position

Frost tolerant no

Soil pH 5.5–6.5

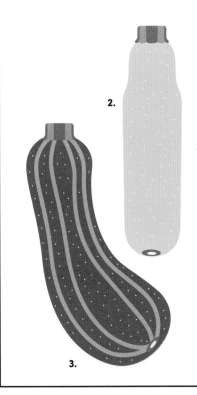

2.

3.

Varieties

Black Coral – dark glossy fruit, compact habit makes it a good choice when space is limited
Golden Zebra – slender, golden fruit with great flavour
Costata Romanesco – very productive, heirloom variety with ribbed fruit that looks like stars when sliced into disks, can be grown on a trellis

Nurture

Sow seeds directly and plant seedlings in spring and summer. Plant into soil that has lots of well-rotted manure and compost added, and mulch around seedlings. Leave around 90 cm (3 feet) between plants. Water regularly.

Flavour companions

basil, capers, coriander, garlic, lemon, mint, oregano, parsley, tomato, walnut

Ways to preserve

pickled, relish

How to use

sandwiches, cheese boards, antipasto, salads

Bread and butter pickles

This sweet and sour pickle is a welcome and efficient response to the inevitable glut of zucchini that occurs every summer, no matter how few plants I grow. Be sure to pick the zucchini when they are small, preferably about 10 cm (4 inches) long.

Place the zucchini and onion in a non-reactive bowl, sprinkle with the salt and toss to coat. Leave to soak for 3 hours.

Shortly before vegetable soaking time is up, prepare the brine. Remove the peel from the lime with a vegetable peeler and slice it into very fine julienne. Squeeze the lime to extract 2 tablespoons of juice.

Combine all the brine ingredients and 125 ml (½ cup) water in a saucepan and bring to the boil.

Pack the zucchini and onion mixture into two or three warm sterilised 250 ml (8½ fl oz) jars (see page 15), leaving 2.5 cm (1 inch) headspace. Fill the jars with the hot brine, leaving 1 cm (½ inch) headspace. Remove any air bubbles by gently running a small spatula down and around the side of the jars. Wipe the rims, seal the jars and process in a water bath for 10 minutes (see page 14). Leave the pickles in a cool, dark place for 4 weeks before using, then refrigerate after opening.

500 g (1 lb 2 oz) small, slender zucchini (courgettes), finely sliced crossways
1 onion, finely sliced
2 tablespoons fine salt

Brine
1 large lime
400 ml (13½ fl oz) apple cider vinegar
150 g (5½ oz) sugar
¼ teaspoon ground turmeric
4 whole cloves
¼ teaspoon celery seeds
2 tablespoons yellow mustard seeds
¼ teaspoon chilli flakes

2–3 x 250 ml (8½ fl oz) sterilised jars

Tomatoes

Solanum lycopersicum

Year after year, tomatoes remind me why I grow and preserve fruits and vegetables. The flavour of freshly picked, sun-warmed tomatoes is above and beyond anything available commercially. With just a few plants you are guaranteed a bountiful supply of fruit at its peak that is sure to provide you with endless preserving inspiration. Jars of bottled tomatoes, rich sauces and flavourful pastes all play their part in a year of cooking.

♈ **Plant** spring, summer

◎ **Harvest** summer, autumn

⚘ **Needs cross-pollination** no

🪴 **Pot** yes

☀ **Aspect** warm, sheltered position

❊ **Frost tolerant** no

⚖ **Soil pH** 5.0–6.5

Tomatoes

1. San Marzano
2. Amish Paste
3. Brandywine

Nurture

Sow seeds into tray filled with seed-raising mix 6–8 weeks before planting out. Seeds need temperatures of 15–30°C (60–85°F) to germinate. Place trays in a warm, sunny position where they are protected from any frosts. Keep seedlings moist (not soggy) and plant out when they are around 5–10 cm (2–4 inches) tall and the risk of frost has passed. It is now possible to find interesting heirloom-variety seedlings in most nurseries, and this is usually how I choose to grow tomatoes.

Tomato seedlings should be planted into soil that has well-rotted manure and compost added. Avoid planting into the same bed in successive years as this will increase the risk of disease. Prepare the soil well ahead of planting so that it is not too rich (over-rich soil tends to produce straggly plants with lots of leaves, but little fruit). Seedlings can be planted very deeply – with 4–5cm (1½–2 inches) of the stalk buried – to encourage root development on their stems. Place stakes or tomato cages in the ground when planting. I use sturdy wooden stakes wrapped with garden string to make a multi-levelled support that winds across the garden bed between multiple plants. Add a layer of mulch; keep plants well watered but avoid watering foliage. When flowers appear, apply a high-potash fertiliser, and then feed fortnightly with a liquid fertiliser.

Flavour companions
basil, capsicum, chilli, chives, cucumber, garlic, ginger, onion, oregano

Ways to preserve
bottled, chutney, paste, puree, relish, sauce

How to use
pasta, stews, soups, cheese boards, with grilled meat

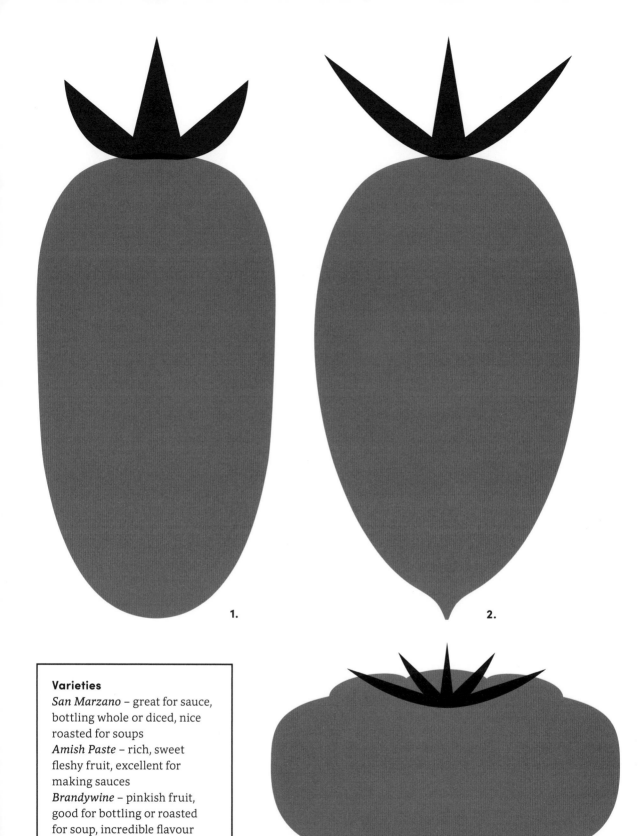

Varieties

San Marzano – great for sauce, bottling whole or diced, nice roasted for soups

Amish Paste – rich, sweet fleshy fruit, excellent for making sauces

Brandywine – pinkish fruit, good for bottling or roasted for soup, incredible flavour

1.

2.

3.

Roasted tomato concentrate

Makes about 4 cups

Roasting intensifies and sweetens the flavour of tomatoes. Made with onion, capsicum and garlic, this concentrated puree is a versatile pantry standby, great tossed through pasta, smeared over a pizza base or made into a comforting soup. Tomatoes have a surprisingly low acid content and must have citric acid added if they are to be preserved safely.

Preheat the oven to 200°C (400°F).

Cut the tomatoes in half and place them, cut side up, on a baking tray, along with the onion and capsicum. Drizzle the olive oil over the top and season with salt and pepper. Roast for 30 minutes, then add the garlic, thyme and basil, tucking them between the softening tomatoes. Roast for another 30 minutes or until everything is jammy and slightly charred on the edges.

Discard all or most of the onion (it has done its job of imparting flavour) and pass the remaining tomato mixture through the fine disc of a food mill (or process in a blender and pass through a fine sieve).

Of course, you can use the concentrated puree straightaway, but if you want to preserve it, reheat the tomato mixture in a clean saucepan until boiling and stir in ½ teaspoon citric acid for every litre (quart) of puree. Fill four or five warm sterilised 250 ml (8½ fl oz) jars (see page 15), leaving 1 cm (½ inch) headspace. Wipe the rims, seal the jars and process in a water bath for 35 minutes (see page 14). Store in a cool, dark place, then refrigerate after opening. Use any leftovers within 2 days.

500 g (1 lb 2 oz) tomatoes, washed and drained
1 onion, quartered
½ red capsicum (pepper), seeds removed, roughly chopped
2 tablespoons olive oil
salt and freshly ground pepper
5 garlic cloves, unpeeled
2–3 thyme sprigs
handful of basil leaves
citric acid (if bottling)

4–5 x 250 ml (8½ fl oz) sterilised jars

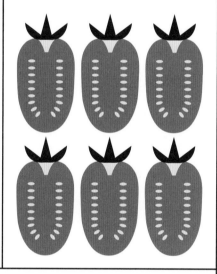

To make a simple tomato soup

Heat the tomato concentrate in a saucepan with some good chicken stock (I use 1 part tomato to 2 parts stock). Stir through a drizzle of balsamic vinegar, then taste and adjust the seasoning if needed. Delicious served with toasted cheese sandwiches.

Capsicums (peppers) *Capsicum annuum*

Homemade pizza is a Friday tradition in our house. I make a big batch of dough and then lay out a choice of toppings; capsicum is a favourite with everyone, so having a ready supply is essential. Capsicums are easy to grow and can be picked when green or red. Plant red, yellow and orange varieties to create jars of multicoloured ribbons. Fruit pickled and processed in a water bath will keep unopened for a year. Roasted strips packed into olive oil and vinegar should always be stored in the refrigerator, where they will keep for around 3 months.

Plant spring, summer

Harvest summer, autumn

Needs cross-pollination no

Pot yes

Aspect full sun

Frost tolerant no

Soil pH 5.5–6.0

Capsicums

1. Gilboa Orange
2. Red Cherry
3. Golden Marconi

Varieties
Gilboa Orange – large, tangerine-coloured fruit with thick, juicy flesh
Red Cherry – small, heart-shaped fruit that looks great when pickled whole
Golden Marconi – green to bright yellow fruit that sweetens as it ripens, grows up to 20 cm (8 inches) long

Nurture
Sow seeds into trays of seed-raising mix, place in a warm, sheltered position and keep moist. After 3–4 weeks, seedlings can be pricked out and transplanted into individual pots. Keep moist and plant out spaced at 45 cm (18 inches) when seedlings are 10 cm (4 inches) tall, or when all risk of frost has passed. Add well-rotted manure to garden before planting out. Plants can break under the weight of their fruit – staking when planting can reduce this risk. Keep plants moist (but not wet), water deeply every second day during hot weather. Apply a layer of mulch to reduce water loss and feed with a balanced liquid fertiliser weekly. Pick fruit using secateurs to protect the plant and to encourage continued fruit production.

Flavour companions
capers, eggplant, garlic, green beans, lemon, olive, onion, tomato

Ways to preserve
pickled, sauce, roasted and preserved in oil

How to use
antipasto, pizza, salads, stews

1.

2.

3.

Pickled capsicum

Makes about 4 cups

I like to make this with a mixture of red, yellow and orange capsicum, but it's fine to be guided by what is ripe and ready to use. The garlic comes down to personal taste – leave it unsliced if you prefer, and feel free to reduce the quantity for a more subtle flavour.

6 capsicums (peppers)
5 garlic cloves, sliced, or to taste
750 ml (1½ pints) apple cider vinegar
2 teaspoons fine salt
1 teaspoon sugar

4–5 x 250 ml (8½ fl oz) sterilised jars

Scorch the capsicums over an open flame or under a grill until the skins are blackened and blistered. Place them in a plastic bag or sealed container for 5–10 minutes to sweat, then peel off the skins, remove the seeds and cut the flesh into strips. Make the strips as large or small as you like. Pack the capsicum strips and garlic into four or five warm sterilised 250 ml (8½ fl oz) jars (see page 15), leaving 2.5 cm (1 inch) headspace.

Combine the vinegar, salt, sugar and 250 ml (1 cup) water in a saucepan and bring to the boil. Pour the liquid over the capsicum and garlic, leaving 1 cm (½ inch) headspace. Remove any air bubbles by gently running a small spatula down and around the side of the jars. Wipe the rims, seal the jars and process in a water bath for 15 minutes (see page 14). Leave the pickles in a cool, dark place for 4 weeks before using, then refrigerate after opening.

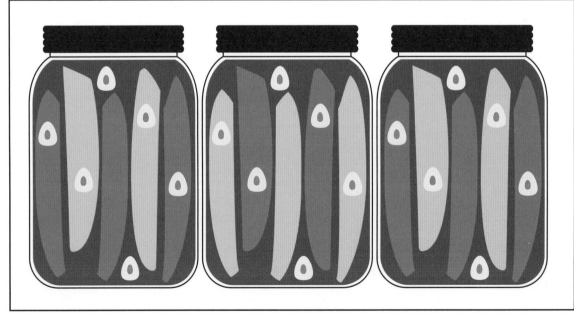

Capsicum preserved in oil

Makes about 2 cups

You can use any colour capsicum for this recipe – the red, yellow and orange varieties will give a sweeter result, but I also like the slightly grassy flavour of green capsicums.

4 capsicums (peppers)
2 tablespoons freshly squeezed lemon juice
500 ml (1 pint) olive oil (approx.)

1 x 500 ml (1 pint) sterilised jar

Scorch the capsicums over an open flame or under a grill until the skins are blackened and blistered. Place them in a plastic bag or sealed container for 5–10 minutes to sweat, then peel off the skins, remove the seeds and cut the flesh into strips. Make the strips as large or small as you like.

Toss the strips and lemon juice in a bowl, then pack into a warm sterilised 500 ml (1 pint) jar (see page 15), adding any lemon juice left in the bowl. Sit the packed jar on a tea towel. Heat the oil until it is shimmering (around 150°C/300°F), then very carefully pour enough over the capsicum mixture to cover it by 1 cm (½ inch). Seal the jars and allow to cool, then store in the fridge for up to 3 months.

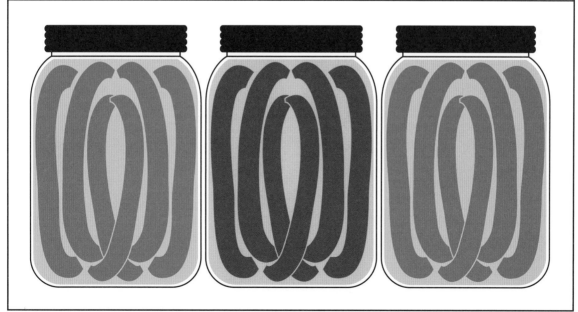

Chillies

Capsicum frutescens

Chillies always feel like a good gardening investment. One or two plants will keep you supplied for months and produce enough fruit to preserve. They can be dried and finely chopped (with or without seeds) to make pepper flakes, preserved in brine, or made into a fiery, sweet jelly or jam.

Plant spring

Harvest summer, autumn

Needs cross-pollination no

Pot yes

Aspect full sun

Frost tolerant no

Soil pH 5.5–7.0

Varieties
Maui Purple – beautiful purple and green foliage surrounding masses of purple fruit that turns red as it ripens and becomes hotter, excellent choice for growing in a pot, will produce into winter
Poblano – dark green fruit that ripens to a brownish-red, mild in flavour
Jalapeño – great multi-purpose chilli, easy to grow, will thrive in a pot; fruit can be pickled, stuffed, and used in sauces

Nurture
Sow seeds in late winter into trays filled with seed-raising mix, keep them in a warm position to encourage germination (you may want to use a heating mat) and water with a spray bottle to keep moist. Covering the trays with glass or a plastic bag will improve humidity, help maintain temperature and reduce moisture loss. Plant seedlings spaced at 30–40 cm (1–1½ feet) apart once the risk of frost has passed. Dig soil deeply and boost the available supply of magnesium and calcium by adding dolomite to the soil before planting. Keep plants well watered and feed every 2 weeks with a high-potash liquid fertiliser. Pick fruit regularly, cut with secateurs to avoid damaging the plant and to encourage continued production.

Flavour companions
coriander, cumin, garlic, ginger, lime, tomato

Ways to preserve
jam, jelly, pickled, dried

How to use
cheese boards, sandwiches, stews, salads

Chillies

1. Maui Purple
2. Poblano
3. Jalapeño

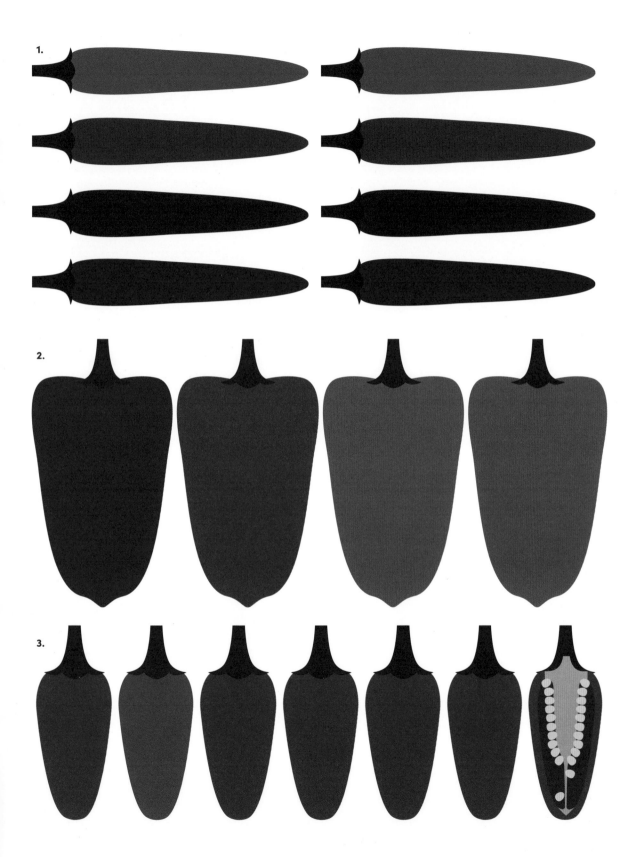

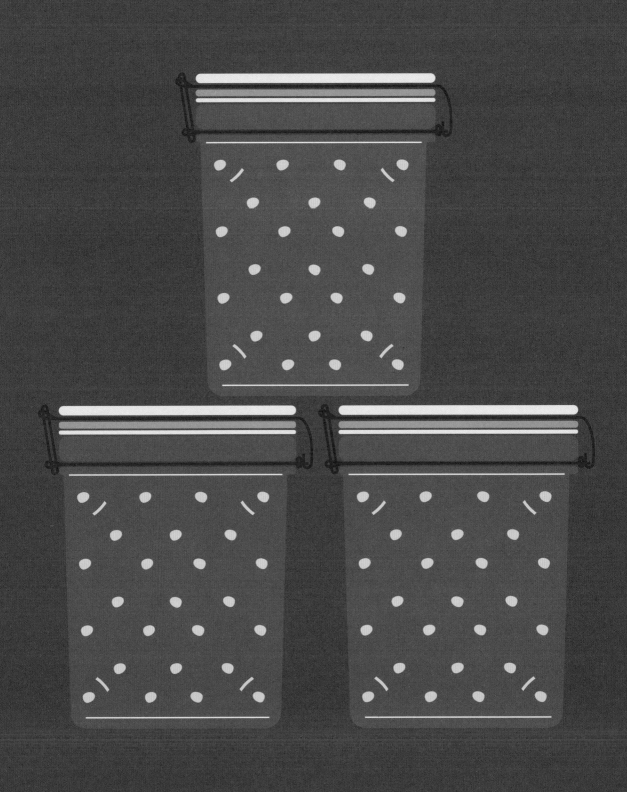

Chilli, lime and mandarin jelly

Makes about 2 cups

The balance of sweet, citrus and heat make this jelly fantastic with a sharp cheddar and even better with peanut butter. It does not achieve a strong set; if you prefer a firm result, add 1 tablespoon of powdered pectin along with the sugar.

....

Remove the peel from the limes with a vegetable peeler and slice it into a very fine julienne, then set aside in small bowl. Squeeze the limes and mandarins, reserving the juice and pips. Pour a little of the juice over the lime zest, cover and keep in the fridge until needed. Remove the pulp from limes and mandarins and tie it in a small square of muslin along with the reserved pips.

Roughly chop the apples, including the skin and core.

Measure out 3 tablespoons of sliced chilli and store, covered, in the fridge until needed. Place the remaining chilli in a heavy-based saucepan, along with the apple, juice, the muslin bag of pips and pulp and 750 ml (1½ pints) water. Cover and cook over medium heat for 20 minutes or until the apple has softened. Remove the muslin bag, pressing it against the side of the pan to extract as much pectin as possible.

Pour the mixture into a square of clean muslin sitting in a colander, then gather up the sides and suspend over a bowl, leaving it to drip overnight. Resist the temptation to squeeze the fruit mixture as this will produce a cloudy jelly.

Place a small saucer in the freezer.

Measure the extracted liquid in the bowl and return it to a clean heavy-based saucepan with 50 g (1¾ oz) sugar for every 100 ml (3½ fl oz) of the liquid. Cook, stirring, over low heat until the sugar has dissolved. Add the reserved chilli and lime zest, increase the heat and cook at a rolling boil for 15–20 minutes until a set is achieved. To test, remove the pan from the heat and place a spoonful of jelly on the cold saucer. Pop the saucer back in the freezer for a couple of minutes – if the jelly wrinkles when pushed, it is ready. If not, cook for another 5 minutes and test again. When set is achieved, leave the jelly to sit for a few minutes, then pour into two or three warm sterilised 200 ml (8 fl oz) jars (see page 15), wipe the rims and seal when cold. Refrigerate after opening.

2 limes
4 mandarins
2 Granny Smith apples
250 g (9 oz) chillies, seeds removed, finely sliced
350 g (12½ oz) sugar (approx.)

2–3 x 200 ml (8 fl oz) sterilised jars

Capers

Capparis spinosa

Both the pods and berries of this deciduous perennial are edible. Capers are the buds before they flower, and caperberries are the fruit that forms after flowering. Salted or brined, these intense pops of slightly astringent flavour are the making of many dishes: chicken piccata, potato salad, green bean and capsicum salad, and remoulade.

♈	**Plant** spring
◎	**Harvest** late spring, summer
✄	**Prune** annual, don't prune for the first 2 years
⚥	**Needs cross-pollination** no
♂	**Bears first fruit** second or third year
⏾	**Pot** yes, in a big pot
☀	**Aspect** full sun
❄	**Frost tolerant** no
⚗	**Soil pH** 7.5–8.0

Varieties

Inermis – sprawling shrub with white and purple flowers, spineless variety, good flavour makes it the first choice for culinary use

Piquant – sharp taste, tender, strong flavour

Baby – firm in texture, less aromatic than other varieties, small-sized buds

French – lemony flavour, strong salty taste, small-sized buds

Nurture

Capers will not grow in humid conditions; they need a hot, dry climate and soil with good drainage. Caper seeds can take months to germinate but are far easier to source than potted plants. Seeds should be soaked in warm water for 2–3 days before planting into trays filled with seed-raising mix. Keep seedlings moist and transplant into individual pots when they reach about 5 cm (2 inches) in height. When planting seedlings, dig through some well-rotted manure or compost before planting at a spacing of 1 m (3 feet). Seedlings and potted plants should be planted at the same level as the soil in the pot. Keep plants well watered until established. Once established they are fairly drought-tolerant but should be watered during extended periods of dry weather and high temperatures. Fertilise with pellet fertiliser in spring and autumn. Caper bushes bear their first fruit in the third or fourth year. Prune annually after the first 2 years; in late autumn or winter remove 5–15 cm (2–6 inches) of growth.

Flavour companions

basil, chilli, citrus, dill, eggplant, green beans, parsley

Ways to preserve

brined, salted

How to use

Add these zesty little pops to potato or green bean salads, chicken dishes, or fish (especially smoked salmon).

Salted or brined capers

Fresh capers are incredibly bitter and must be salted or brined before eating.

Salted capers

Pick caper pods that are firm, place them in a bowl and cover with salt. Leave to cure in a cool, dark place for 10 days, stirring occasionally and pouring off any liquid that accumulates. After 10 days, add more salt and leave for another 10 days. Drain and weigh the capers – the quantity of salt you need for packing is 20 per cent of the caper weight. Layer the capers with salt in warm sterilised jars (see page 15), wipe the rims and seal. Rinse before using and refrigerate after opening.

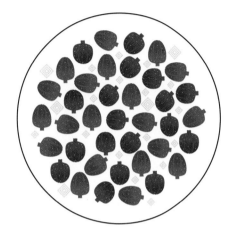

Brined capers

Place the capers in a clean jar, cover with water and seal. Leave for 24 hours, then drain and cover with fresh water. Repeat this process three more times (four rounds of soaking in total). To make a brine, combine equal parts white wine vinegar and water in a saucepan and add 1 tablespoon fine salt for every 250 ml (1 cup) liquid. Bring to the boil, stirring until the salt has dissolved, then remove from the heat and cool for about 20 minutes. Place the drained capers in a warm sterilised jar (see page 15) and pour over the brine, leaving 1 cm (½ inch) headspace. Wipe the rims, seal the jars and process in a water bath for 10 minutes (see page 14). Leave in a cool, dark place for 4 weeks, then refrigerate after opening.

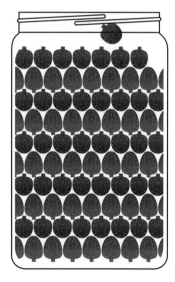

Pickled caperberries

Caperberries need to be soaked before they are used in this recipe. The quantities given here are a guide only and, providing you retain the ratios of water, vinegar and salt, you can make your batch as large or small as you like.

160 g (1 cup) caperberries
250 ml (1 cup) white wine vinegar
2 tablespoons fine salt
juice of 1 lemon

Soak the caperberries in cold water for 3 days, changing the water daily.

Place the vinegar, salt and 250 ml (1 cup) water in a saucepan and bring to the boil, stirring until the salt has dissolved. Add the lemon juice and return to the boil.

Drain the caperberries and pack them into warm sterilised jars, leaving 2.5 cm (1 inch) headspace. Cover with the hot brine, leaving 1 cm (½ inch) headspace. Wipe the rims, seal the jars and process in a water bath for 10 minutes (see page 14). Leave in a cool, dark place for at least 1 week, then refrigerate after opening. Caperberries may be rinsed before using.

Garlic

Allium sativum

I grow garlic to have a ready supply for various sauces and chutney, and so I don't have to deal with the ghastly stale or imported bulbs that dominate the greengrocers' shelves. Because garlic keeps well tied into bunches or twisted into plaits and hung in a well-ventilated place, the idea of preserving it seems unnecessary. But having a small ready-to-go supply of roasted garlic is a persuasive argument for doing so.

⚘	**Plant** autumn
◎	**Harvest** spring, early summer
⚘	**Needs cross-pollination** no
⊍	**Pot** yes, in deep tubs or troughs
☀	**Aspect** full sun
❋	**Frost tolerant** yes
⏚	**Soil pH** 6.8–7.5

Varieties
Valiant – flattened, globe-shaped bulbs with purplish skin and plump cloves, early cropping, crisp garlic flavour
Dynamite Purple – late cropping variety with dark pinkish-purple cloves, hot garlic flavour, great for plaiting and storing
White Crookneck – mildly-flavoured variety with white cloves and skin, easy to grow

Nurture
Plant individual cloves 10 cm (4 inches) apart into well-drained soil that has been enriched with well-rotted manure, compost and rock dust, or blood and bone. Choose plump cloves and place them at a depth of 5 cm (2 inches) with their tips pointing upwards. Water and mulch with a 10 cm (4 inch) layer of straw. When shoots appear, apply liquid fertiliser every 2 weeks and keep moist, but not waterlogged. Bulbs are ready to harvest when most leaves have died and only two to three green leaves remain. Hang bunches of bulbs out of direct sunlight in a cool place with good ventilation for 1–2 months to allow skins to harden.

Flavour companions
basil, capsicum, fennel, parsley, potato, tomato

Ways to preserve
dried, frozen, butter, paste

How to use
stews, sauces, marinades, for basting meats

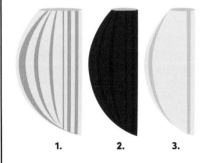

Garlic

1. Valiant
2. Dynamite Purple
3. White Crookneck

Roasted garlic paste

*Despite bunches of garlic hanging in the garage, I seem to need roasted garlic when
I don't have the time or inclination to wait an hour while the cloves transform into a rich,
delicious paste. Freezing this paste is a quick solution and a brilliant way to make use
of a bumper crop. Mix it with butter to make garlic bread, add it to soups and stews or
pop it into the cavity of a chicken before roasting.*

Preheat the oven to 200°C (400°F).

Slice the tops off the garlic bulbs and drizzle with a little olive oil. Tightly wrap
individual bulbs in lightly oiled foil and place them on a baking tray, then roast for
40–60 minutes until the flesh has softened and turned a beautiful golden colour.
Allow the bulbs to cool slightly, then squeeze the flesh into a bowl and mix with a
fork to make a smooth paste. Spoon into ice cube trays, or drop teaspoons of paste
onto a tray lined with baking paper, and freeze. Transfer the frozen blocks to an
airtight bag or container and store in the freezer for up to 12 months.

Ginger

Zingiber officinale

Success in growing ginger depends on a tropical climate and a warm, partially-shaded position. A deciduous perennial in its natural environment, ginger can be grown as an annual in cooler climates. This edible rhizome's hot, sweet, and spicy flavour is indispensable in chutneys and relishes. Freshly harvested ginger can be pickled or peeled and preserved in sherry – but my favourite use is ginger beer.

⚘	**Plant** rhizomes in early spring
◎	**Harvest** late autumn, winter
❦❦	**Needs cross-pollination** no
⛫	**Pot** yes
☀	**Aspect** part sun
❄	**Frost tolerant** no
⌁	**Soil pH** 5.5–6.5

Varieties

Zingiber officinale – the most common form of edible ginger

Always check before planting ginger that it is of the edible variety.

Nurture

Look for a fresh ginger root with developing buds. Plant this just below the surface of a seed tray filled with potting mix and leave in a warm place until shoots have developed. Transplant to a large pot or straight into the garden; planting it in a warm, sheltered position and into soil that has compost and a small amount of sand worked through. Keep plants moist and feed with a liquid fertiliser every 2 weeks. Plants die down in autumn, at which time dead leaves should be removed and roots can be harvested. Save and replant any roots that have sprouted.

Flavour companions

basil, beans, chilli, coriander, cumin, garlic, lemon, lime, mint, orange, rhubarb, turmeric

Ways to preserve

candied, dried, cordial, in sherry

How to use

dried – soups, stews; candied – baking; preserved in sherry – in stir-fry

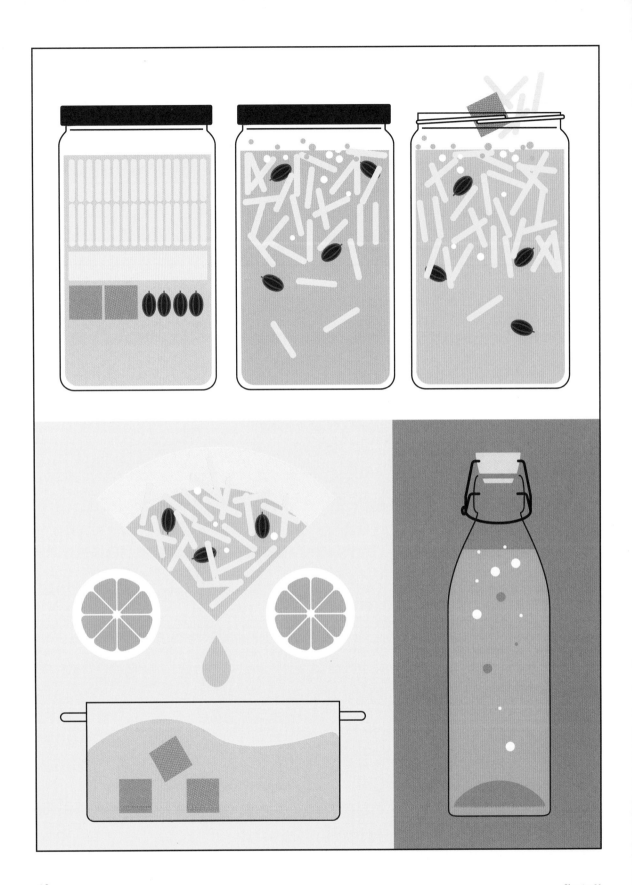

Ginger beer

Homemade ginger beer is fermented and therefore a lively concoction. Always take great care when opening bottles; point the tops away from yourself and anyone around you. If you don't have enough homegrown ginger, feel free to use a mixture of fresh and ground ginger when feeding the 'plant' – 1 tablespoon grated fresh ginger is equal to ¼ teaspoon ground ginger. Young, freshly picked ginger does not need peeling; just give it a good wash before grating.

Ginger beer plant

Place all the plant ingredients in a sterilised 1 litre (1 quart) jar (see page 15) and seal. Leave at room temperature out of direct sunlight for 3–4 days to ferment – by this time you should see small bubbles on the surface of the liquid. If not, leave it for a few more days.

Feed the plant with 60 g (⅓ cup) freshly grated ginger and 2 teaspoons sugar each day for the next 7–14 days. During this time air pockets will form, making the mixture look like a sponge. If this doesn't happen, don't give up; just keep feeding the plant daily until you see a change. Cooler temperatures can delay the process, and I usually find the first plant comes to life much more slowly than subsequent plants.

Ginger beer plant
60 g (⅓ cup) freshly grated ginger
4 sultanas (golden raisins)
juice of 1 lemon
2 teaspoons sugar
250 ml (1 cup) cold distilled water

To feed the plant
freshly grated ginger
sugar

To make the ginger beer

Place the sugar in a large heatproof bowl or jug, pour over the boiling water and stir until the sugar has dissolved. Stir in the lemon juice, then add the ginger plant and mix well. Strain through a muslin cloth into a large bowl, squeezing to extract all the liquid. Reserve about a cup of the ginger pulp that remains in the muslin and use it to start another plant, feeding it with sugar and ginger as described above.

Combine the ginger liquid with 3.5 litres (3½ quarts) water and pour into warm sterilised bottles (see page 15). Seal, then leave to rest in a cool, dark place for at least 3 days before using.

400 g (14 oz) sugar
500 ml (1 pint) boiling water
juice of 2 lemons, or to taste

Beetroot

Beta vulgaris

Beetroot is a delight to grow at home, with a wide range of colours, sizes and shapes to brighten up any preserving garden. It also allows you to harvest this earthy root vegetable when they are small and sweet. I preserve sliced, wedged and whole beetroots in a lightly spiced brine. The multicoloured display is as pleasing as the reliable supply of beetroot, ready to be used in countless ways.

♈	**Plant** year-round in most areas
◎	**Harvest** year-round
⚤	**Needs cross-pollination** no
⊽	**Pot** yes, in deep tubs or troughs
☼	**Aspect** full sun
✳	**Frost tolerant** yes
⏚	**Soil pH** 6.5–7.0

Varieties

Burpee's Golden – sweet baby beet with golden-yellow flesh when cooked
Mini Gourmet – dark red, golf-ball-sized beets with intense flavour; grows well in containers and a good choice for summer planting
Chioggia – tender, mild and sweet beets with concentric circles of alternating pink and white, impressive when sliced and pickled

Nurture

Soak seeds overnight before planting direct into soil with good drainage and plenty of well-rotted compost worked through. Water regularly during germination and thin seedlings to 10 cm (4 inch) spacing. Beets can be harvested as soon as they reach the size of a golf ball, or can be left to mature to the size of a tennis ball (any larger than this and the beet is likely to split, be woody in texture and less flavourful).

Flavour companions

almond, allspice, apple, basil, blueberry, caraway seeds, carrot, cinnamon, coriander, cucumber, cumin, dill, fennel, garlic, lemon, mint, orange, paprika, parsley, pepper, tarragon, thyme, walnut

Ways to preserve

pickled

How to use

salads, burgers, charcuterie

Beetroot

1. Burpee's Golden
2. Mini Gourmet
3. Chioggia

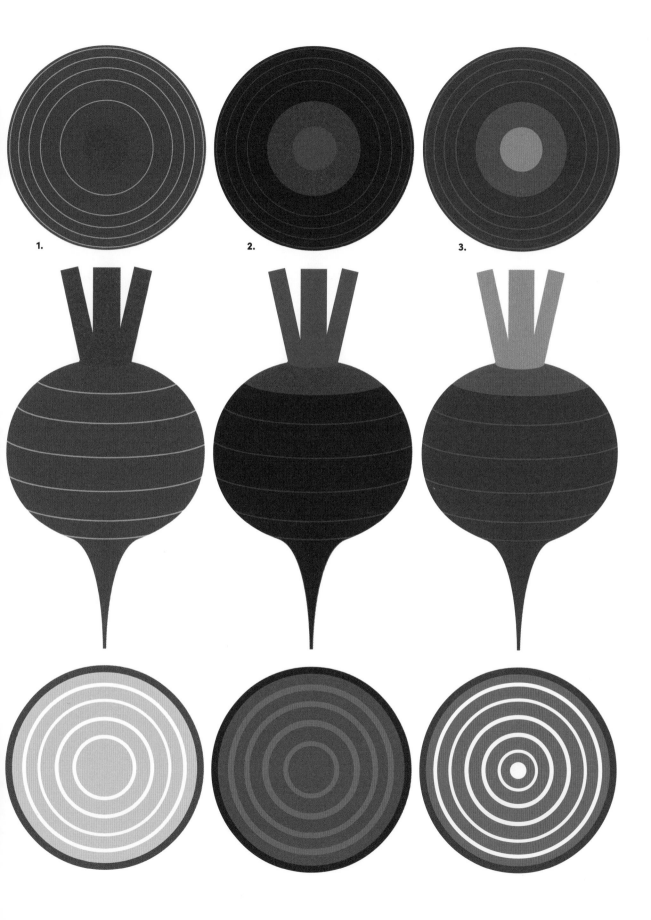

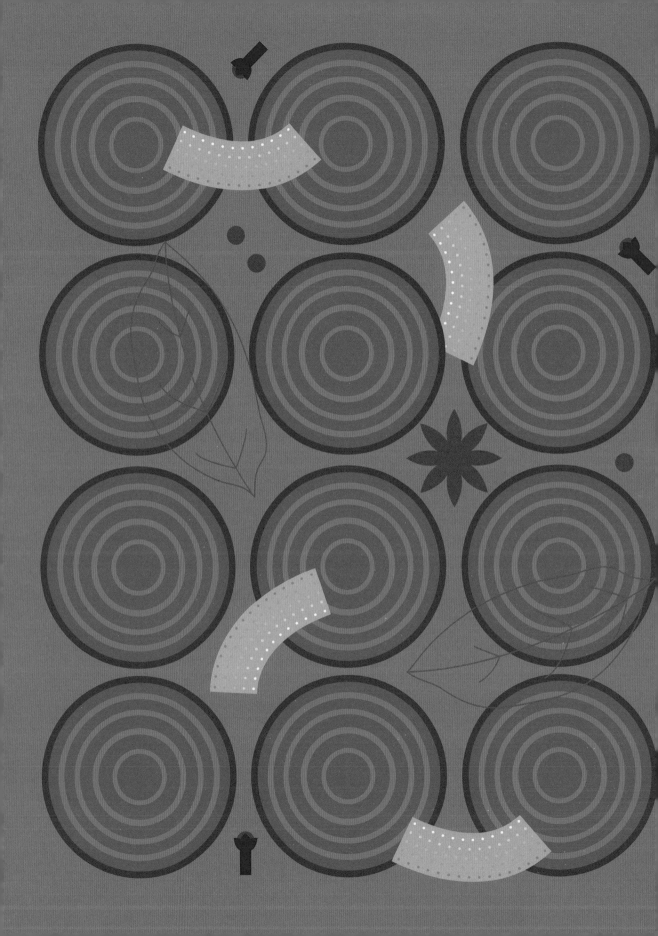

Pickled beetroot

Essential in a burger and fantastic tossed through a salad, this pickle balances warm spices, zesty orange and the tang of apple cider vinegar with the sweet, earthy flavour of beetroot.

....

Preheat the oven to 160°C (315°F).

Wash and trim the beetroot, leaving the long root and around 2 cm (¾ inch) of stalk attached. Wrap the bulbs in individual foil parcels and place them on a baking tray. Roast for 1¼ hours or until tender. Remove and set aside to cool slightly.

Wearing gloves, peel the beetroot and cut into slices or wedges. Pack into four warm sterilised 300 ml (10 fl oz) jars (see page 15), adding a strip of orange rind to each jar.

Combine the vinegar, spices, salt, sugars, remaining orange rind and 200 ml (7 fl oz) water in a saucepan and bring to the boil, stirring until the sugars have dissolved. Pour over the beetroot, leaving 1 cm (½ inch) headspace. Remove any air bubbles by gently running a small spatula down and around the side of the jars. Wipe the rims, seal the jars and process in a water bath for 30 minutes (see page 14). Leave the pickled beetroot in a cool, dark place for at least 3–4 weeks before using, then refrigerate after opening.

l kg (2 lb 3 oz) beetroot
6 strips of orange rind, pith removed
400 ml (13½ fl oz) apple cider vinegar
3 whole cloves
2 whole allspice
2 bay leaves
1 star anise
3 whole black peppercorns
½ teaspoon fine salt
50 g (1¾ oz) sugar
30 g (1 oz) brown sugar

4 x 300 ml (10 fl oz) sterilised jars

Carrots

Daucus carota

Carrots are a touchstone for vegetable growing, and one of my favourites. There is no store-bought carrot that can match the bright, earthy sweetness of a carrot freshly picked, washed off under the garden tap and eaten with the leafy top still attached. Don't let limited space or even the lack of a garden bed put you off growing carrots. A large, deep trough is a perfect container for growing these sweet root vegetables.

♈	**Plant** sow seeds direct in spring
◎	**Harvest** spring, summer, autumn
❦❦	**Needs cross-pollination** no
☐	**Pot** yes, in deep tubs or troughs
☼	**Aspect** full sun
✳	**Frost tolerant** yes
⏚	**Soil pH** 6.0–7.0

Varieties
St Valery – reliable and productive French heirloom; long, sweet orange–red roots
Baby Amsterdam – dwarf variety with compact foliage, suitable for close planting

Nurture
Carrots should be grown in deep, rich, light loamy soil. Add blood and bone or well-rotted manure at least 30 cm (1 foot) below the surface 1 to 2 months before planting (soil that is too rich can cause carrots to fork). Sow seeds directly into shallow drills at a depth of 1–2 cm (½–¾ inch). Thin seedlings to around 10 cm (4 inches) apart. Keep soil well weeded.

Flavour companions
caraway seed, celery, coriander seed, dill, fennel, garlic, ginger, mustard, nutmeg, parsley, pepper

Ways to preserve
jam, pickled, puree

How to use
salads, sandwiches, charcuterie, cheese boards, as a tasty side dish

Carrots

1. St Valery
2. Baby Amsterdam

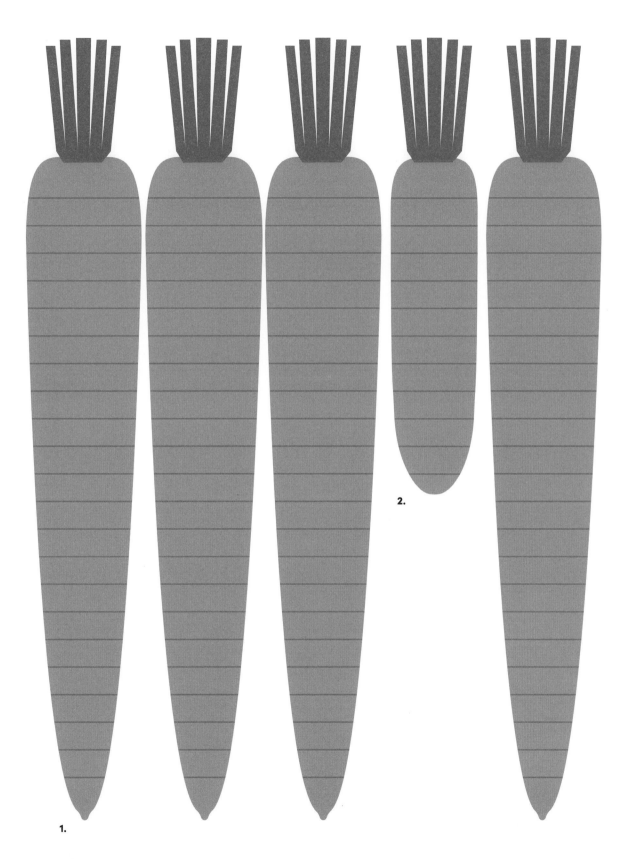

1.

2.

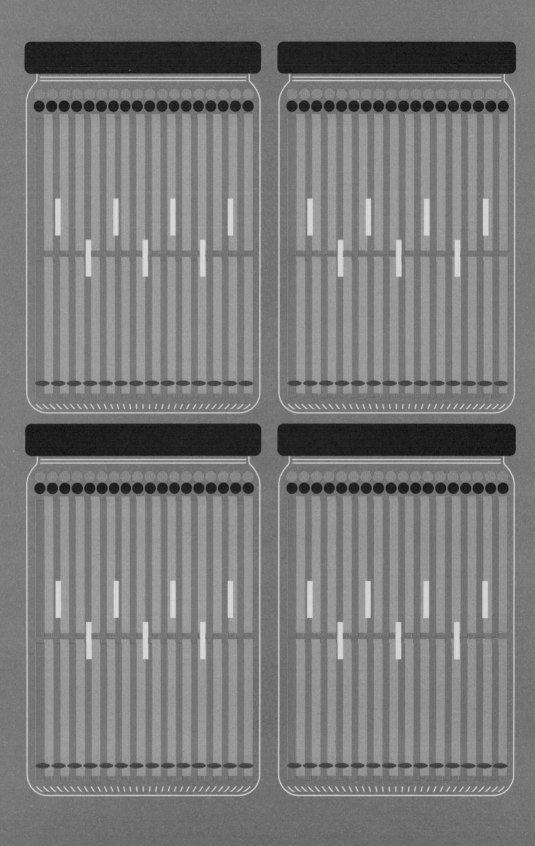

Pickled carrot

Makes about 2½ cups

The texture and balanced sweet-and-sour flavour of this pickled carrot is lovely in a salad and offers a delicious contrast to roasted meats, especially in a pork sandwich. I like to shred the carrots on the fine julienne blade of a mandolin, but you can also cut them very finely by hand.

....

Combine the vinegar, spices, ginger, sugar, salt and 500 ml (1 pint) water in a heavy-based saucepan and bring to the boil, stirring until the sugar has dissolved. Add the carrot and cook for 1 minute, then lift the carrot from the brine with a slotted spoon and pack it into two or three warm sterilised 250 ml (8½ fl oz) jars (see page 15), leaving 2.5 cm (1 inch) headspace.

Return the pickling liquid to the boil, then pour it over the carrot, leaving 1 cm (½ inch) headspace. Remove any air bubbles by gently running a small spatula down and around the side of the jars. Wipe the rims, seal the jars and process in a water bath for 10 minutes (see page 14). Leave the pickled carrot in a cool, dark place for at least 2–3 weeks before using, then refrigerate after opening.

500 ml (1 pint) apple cider vinegar
1½ teaspoons fennel seeds
¼ teaspoon whole black peppercorns
1 teaspoon coriander seeds
2 cm (¾ inch) piece of ginger, peeled and sliced
150 g (5½ oz) sugar
1 teaspoon fine salt
500 g (1 lb 2 oz) carrots, peeled and julienned

2–3 x 250 ml (8½ fl oz) sterilised jars

Fennel

Foeniculum vulgare dulce

The subtle anise flavour and crisp texture of fennel are fantastic in salads. Having a homegrown supply means you can pick bulbs when they are at their peak – tender and bursting with flavour – and avoid the tough, flavourless offerings of the greengrocer. Wild fennel is an invasive weed in many countries; be sure to plant Florence fennel, with its plump overlapping bulbs.

Plant spring, autumn

Harvest late summer, autumn

Needs cross-pollination no

Pot yes, in a big pot

Aspect full sun

Frost tolerant yes

Soil pH 5.5–7.0

Varieties
Florence Zefa Fino – large, quick-growing, crisp, sweet bulbs
Florence Romanesco – broad bulbs with a delicate flavour, late cropping, less prone to bolting than other varieties
Mantovano – mid-sized bulbs with a crisp texture and sweet flavour

Nurture
Prepare soil with the addition of well-rotted manure and compost before planting. Sow seeds directly at a depth of 8mm ($5/16$ inch). Thin seedlings to 30 cm (1 foot). Mulch well, keep plants well watered and apply liquid fertiliser every 2 weeks. When you see the base of the stems begin to swell, mound up soil around them to 'blanch' the bulb (this will prevent the bulb from browning).

Flavour companions
capers, capsicum, chilli, garlic, lemon, olive, orange, tomato, walnut

Ways to preserve
pickled

How to use
salads, served with fish or braised meats

Pickled fennel

Makes about 2 cups

Fennel pickled with orange is a perfect flavour pairing. I often serve it in a salad of rocket, orange segments and finely sliced onion, but it's also delicious as an accompaniment to grilled lamb or cured meats. If you have one, the fine julienne blade on a mandolin makes short work of preparing the fennel.

Place the fennel in a non-reactive bowl, toss with the salt and lemon juice and leave to sit for 1 hour. Drain any liquid from the bowl, then stir in the orange zest. Pack into two warm sterilised 300 ml (10 fl oz) jars (see page 15), along with the reserved fennel fronds, leaving 2 cm (¾ inch) headspace.

Combine the orange juice, vinegar, sugar and peppercorns in a saucepan and bring to the boil, stirring until the sugar has dissolved. Pour the pickling liquid over the fennel, leaving 1 cm (½ inch) headspace.

Remove any air bubbles by gently running a small spatula down and around the side of the jars. Wipe the rims, seal the jars and process in a water bath for 15 minutes (see page 14). Leave the pickle in a cool, dark place for 3–4 weeks before using, then refrigerate after opening.

2 fennel bulbs, trimmed and julienned, fronds reserved
1 teaspoon fine salt
juice of ½ lemon
grated zest of 1 orange
200 ml (7 fl oz) freshly squeezed orange juice
200 ml (7 fl oz) apple cider vinegar
2 teaspoons sugar
4 whole black peppercorns, lightly cracked

2 x 300 ml (10 fl oz) sterilised jars

Cabbage

Brassica oleracea

I associate cabbages with winter, but with planning, it is possible to have cabbage ready for harvest throughout the year. Like all brassicas, cabbages are very hungry feeders and should be grown in soil that has been heavily boosted before planting.

Plant depends on variety

Harvest depends on variety

Needs cross-pollination no

Pot yes, large pot with single plant

Aspect full sun to part shade

Frost tolerant yes

Soil pH 7.5

Varieties
Early Jersey Wakefield – tight cone-shaped heads, suitable for small spaces
Red Drumhead – blue outer leaves and a large, red heart put on a showy display; great multi-purpose cabbage, can be used for coleslaw, fermenting, or tossed in a pan with onion and cherries
Chou de Milan de Pontoise – round, semi-savoy cabbage with leaves displaying shades of green, blue and pink

Nurture
Plant at a spacing of 40–75 cm (1–2½ feet), depending on variety, into fertile, well-drained soil that has been prepared with lots of well-rotted manure and compost. Mulch well after planting, adding all-purpose fertiliser if planting in spring and summer. Keep garden beds weeded and well watered in dry periods. Control cabbage moths with derris dust or pyrethrum.

Flavour companions
apple, beetroot, caraway seeds, carrot, celery, coriander seed, dill, fennel, garlic, ginger, mustard, nutmeg, onion, orange, parsley, potato, sour cherry

Ways to preserve
pickled

How to use
in pork dishes, salads; with baked potatoes, scrambled eggs, avocado toast

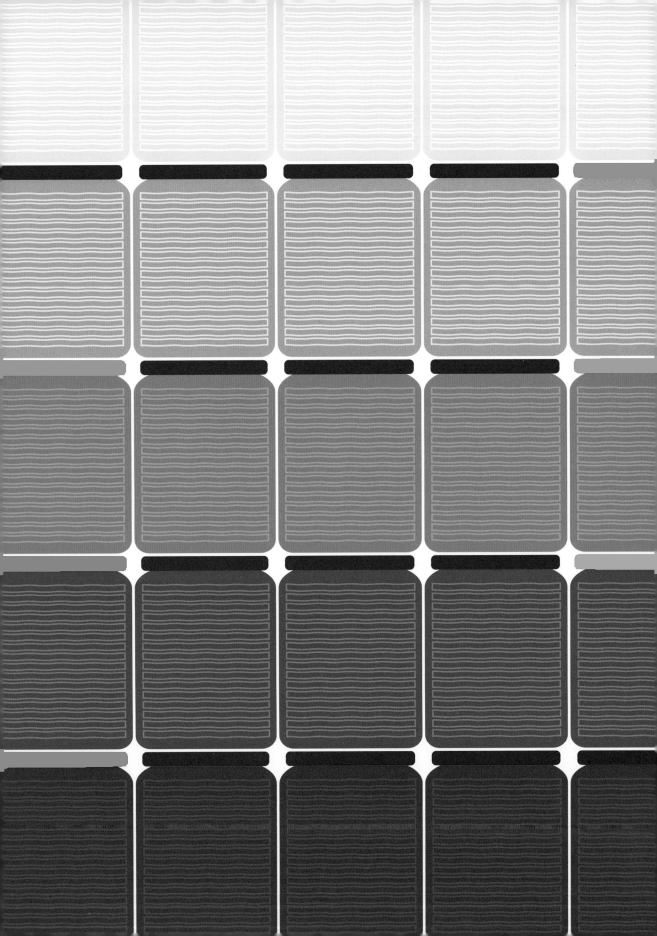

Sunset sauerkraut

I love the vibrant colour that emerges as white cabbage mingles with beetroot and turmeric; it's a beautiful shade of saffron that, like a sunset, deepens as beetroot exerts its power, giving the mixture a darker red hue.

½ white cabbage
1½ tablespoons fine salt
1 carrot
1 small beetroot
1 green apple
1–2 garlic cloves, minced
1 teaspoon freshly grated ginger
1 teaspoon freshly grated turmeric

1 x 1 litre (1 quart) sterilised jar

Remove the outer leaves and wash the cabbage before peeling off and reserving a whole leaf. Cut the cabbage into wedges, remove the core and shred the leaves with a knife or mandolin. Place in a non-reactive bowl, sprinkle with the salt and massage with your hands for 5–10 minutes until the cabbage has softened and released a pool of brine in the bottom of the bowl.

Coarsely grate the carrot and beetroot. Peel the apple and cut it into small batons – a mandolin is the quickest and easiest way to do this. Add the carrot, beetroot, apple, garlic, ginger and turmeric to the cabbage and, wearing gloves to avoid staining, mix everything together.

Pack the mixture into a 1 litre (1 quart) warm sterilised jar (see page 15), pushing it down with your fist, leaving 2.5 cm (1 inch) headspace. Pour in enough of the brine to submerge the cabbage and top with the reserved cabbage leaf to ensure it stays fully covered.

Seal the jar, sit it in a bowl to catch any brine and leave to ferment in a cool place out of direct sunlight. Fermentation time can vary, according to taste. Check the mixture daily and after 1 week, open the jar and try some of the kraut. If the flavour and tang are to your liking, place the jar in the fridge, where it can be stored for a year. If you want a funkier kraut, continue fermenting until it reaches your desired tang.

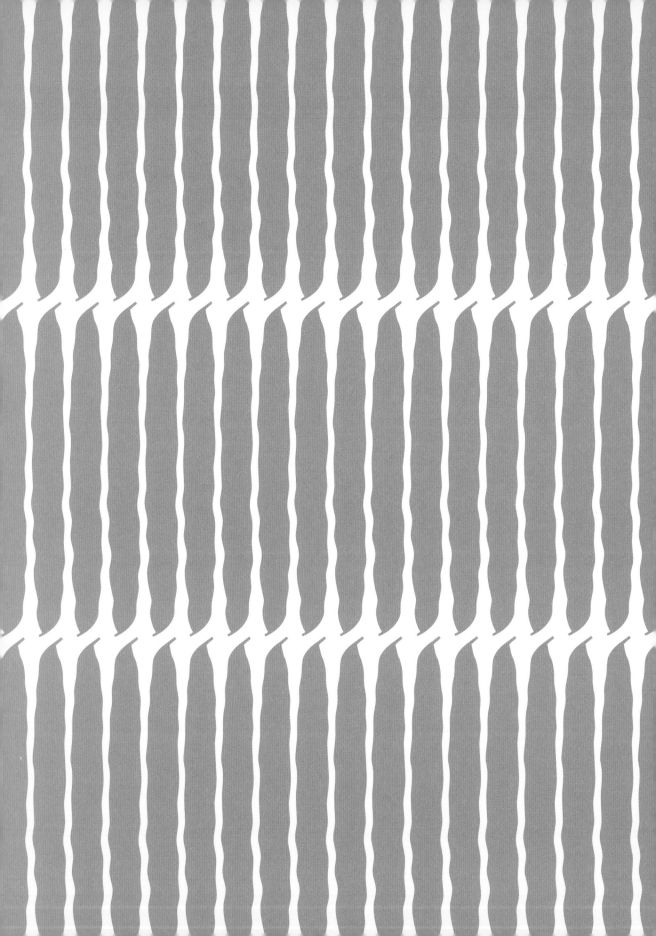

Beans

Phaseolus vulgaris

Beans are a quick-and-easy flavourful addition to any home garden. I typically choose to grow climbing beans – they require less real estate than the bush varieties and add vertical interest to the garden. Plant climbing beans against a wire fence, bamboo tepee or an A-frame constructed using five poles and lengths of garden string. If you plant beans and corn together the beans will supply much-needed nitrogen into the soil, and the corn will structurally support the beans.

𐤀 Plant spring, summer

◎ Harvest midsummer, autumn

⚘ Needs cross-pollination no

▽ Pot yes

☼ Aspect full sun, part shade

✳ Frost tolerant no

⬦ Soil pH 6.5–7.0

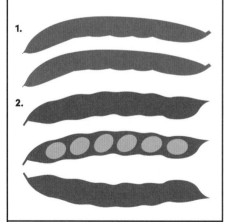

Beans

1. Blue Lake
2. Lazy Housewife
3. Northeaster (opposite)

Varieties

Blue Lake – climbing produces large, flat beans that stand up to the process of bottling
Lazy Housewife – climbing, stringless, high-cropping heirloom variety
Northeaster – long, tender beans with a sweet flavour, stays tender over an extended period

Nurture

Plant beans directly at 20 cm (8 inch) spacing through spring and summer into soil that has been well boosted with rotted manure and compost. Planting beans where hungry brassicas (such as broccoli) have grown will help replenish soil by fixing nitrogen. Once seedlings have emerged, apply a layer of mulch around the base of the plants to keep soil moist. Keep plants watered, and when flowers appear feed with a fortnightly application of liquid fertiliser. Beans are at their most tender if picked when young. Remain vigilant about picking to encourage continued production.

Flavour companions

almond, beetroot, capers, capsicum, celery, chilli, chives, coriander, cumin, garlic, lemon, mint, olive, parsley, pine nut, spring onion, tarragon, tomato

Ways to preserve

pickled, dried, frozen

How to use

salads, sandwiches, charcuterie, antipasto

Giardiniera

*This quick vegetable pickle is a moveable feast and a valuable
way to preserve small quantities of various vegetables.
The amounts given here can be adjusted according to what
you have; just keep the vinegar and water, and the sugar and
salt at a 1:1 ratio.*

Wash all the vegetables and cut them into bite-sized pieces:
divide the cauliflower into small florets, chop the fennel into
2 cm (¾ inch) dice, slice the carrots into rounds, slice the
celery into 2 cm (¾ inch) pieces, cut the green beans in half,
slice the capsicum into strips, and remove the roots and
most of the green from the spring onions.

Combine the vinegar, sugar, salt, peppercorns, bay leaf
and 500 ml (1 pint) water in a large saucepan and bring to
the boil. Add the cauliflower, fennel and carrot and simmer
for 4 minutes, then add the remaining vegetables and
simmer for another 3 minutes. Scoop out all the vegetables
with a slotted spoon and spread them over a tray lined with
paper towel to cool. Reserve the pickling liquid and set it
aside to cool.

Layer the cooled vegetables into five or six warm sterilised
200 ml (7 fl oz) jars (see page 15), leaving 2.5 cm (1 inch)
headspace. Pour in enough of the pickling liquid to cover
the vegetables, leaving 1 cm (½ inch) headspace. Remove
any air bubbles by gently running a small spatula down and
around the side of the jars. Wipe the rims, seal the jars
and process in a water bath for 20 minutes (see page 14).
Refrigerate after opening.

100 g (3½ oz) cauliflower
1 small fennel bulb
1 carrot
1 celery stick
150 g (5½ oz) green beans
1 capsicum (pepper), seeds removed
3–4 spring onions (scallions)
500 ml (1 pint) white wine vinegar
½ teaspoon sugar
½ teaspoon fine salt
3–4 whole peppercorns
1 bay leaf

5–6 x 200 ml (7 fl oz) sterilised jars

1.   2.   3.

Corn

Zea mays

Corn is an excellent crop for children to grow. There is something especially thrilling about the tall stalks and swelling cobs topped with silk that can inspire future gardeners. And, of course, nothing beats the flavour of freshly picked corn when eaten before the sugars have turned to starch. If you want to eat freshly picked corn, put the pot on to boil before harvesting cobs so you can start cooking within minutes.

Plant spring

Harvest late summer, autumn

Needs cross-pollination yes, open-pollinated varieties

Pot no

Aspect full sun

Frost tolerant yes

Soil pH 5.8–7.0

Corn

1. True Gold
2. Country Gentleman
3. Legacy

Varieties
True Gold – open pollination variety, each plant will produce two to three large cobs that are crisp and not overly sweet
Country Gentleman – open pollination, heirloom variety with long white kernels arranged in a 'shoe peg' pattern instead of rows
Legacy – high-yield variety with large yellow cobs, sweet flavour

Nurture
Sow seeds directly, after the risk of frost has passed, into soil that has lots of manure and compost added. Seeds should be planted at a depth of 2–3 cm (¾–1¼ inches) and spaced at 30–40 cm (12–16 inches). I plant seed in a zig-zag pattern to improve pollination, and if possible, into a bed where nitrogen-fixing peas or broad beans have grown. Apply a liquid fertiliser just as plants are about to flower. Male flowers are born at the top of the plant, while female flowers grow along the stalk. If you only grow a few plants, give the stalks a gentle tap to release pollen from the male flowers onto the silk of the female flowers. Mound soil around the base of plants when they are around 30 cm (1 foot) tall and mulch well. Corn is ready to pick when kernels release a milky liquid when pierced, silk is slightly brown and dry, and the cobs feel full and firm.

Flavour companions
butter, capsicum, chilli, coriander, cumin, lime, tomato

Ways to preserve
pickled, chutney, relish

How to use
burgers, salads, antipasto, cheese boards, baked potatoes

Roasted corn relish

Makes about 2 cups

This sweet and tangy relish is a classic burger condiment that also pairs beautifully with cheese and charcuterie. If you have them, finely chopped chilli and diced capsicum both make excellent additions.

Preheat the oven to 220°C (425°F).

Place the corn cobs on a baking tray and roast, turning halfway through, for 40 minutes or until they have browned slightly. Set aside to cool, then slice off the kernels.

Heat the oil in a large saucepan over medium heat and fry the mustard seeds until they begin to pop. Add the shallot and cook, stirring, for a minute or two until softened. Add the corn kernels and all the remaining ingredients, then bring to the boil, stirring frequently, until the mixture has thickened slightly.

Spoon the relish into two warm sterilised 300 ml (10 fl oz) jars (see page 15), leaving 1 cm (½ inch) headspace, and gently tap the jars on the countertop to help it settle. Wipe the rims, seal the jars and process in a water bath for 15 minutes (see page 14). Refrigerate after opening.

6 corn cobs, husks and silks removed
1 tablespoon olive oil
2½ teaspoons yellow mustard seeds
2 small French shallots, finely chopped
200 ml (7 fl oz) brown malt vinegar
350 g (12½ oz) tomatoes, peeled (see page 16), seeds removed, finely chopped
1 teaspoon fine salt
1 teaspoon brown sugar
pinch of saffron threads (optional)
freshly ground pepper

2 x 300 ml (10 fl oz) sterilised jars

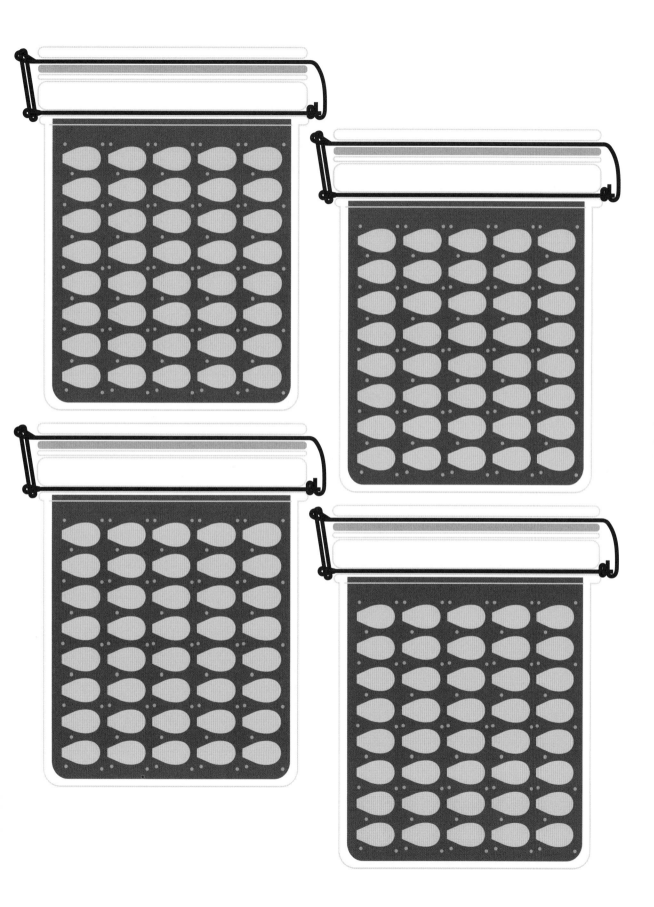

Rhubarb

Rheum rhabarbarum

I love rhubarb: rhubarb and strawberry crumble, rhubarb pie, roasted strawberries and rhubarb on top of a pavlova – the list goes on. This vegetable is so easy to grow that I regularly divide crowns to give away or discard to make room in the garden. One or two plants produce enough crimson stalks for crumbles and a supply of frozen stewed fruit, and still leave me looking for other ways to use the crop.

Plant crowns in late autumn, winter

Harvest year-round, best in autumn

Needs cross-pollination yes

Pot yes

Aspect open, sunny position

Frost tolerant yes

Soil pH 5.5–6.5

Varieties
Victoria – old variety, named after Queen Victoria, produces large, intensely red stalks with good flavour
Winter Wonder – cold-tolerant with luminous red stalks, available when other varieties are cut back over winter
Ruby Red – dwarf, bright red, compact variety with short thick stems, great for growing in containers

Nurture
Rhubarb thrives in deep, rich and well-drained sandy soil. Before planting, work in plenty of well-rotted manure or compost and a complete fertiliser. Plant crowns around 60 cm (2 feet) apart. Water well in dry periods. Resist picking all the stalks in the first year after planting, this allows the plant to become well established and increases yields in subsequent years. Cut off any flower heads that appear. Apply an annual dressing of compost or manure in late autumn or early winter, gently forking it in around the roots. In early spring, mulch around crowns with a mixture of compost and manure. Plants can be divided every 3–4 years. Pick stems by twisting them from the plant. Remove any old, dead stalks as they appear.

Flavour companions
cinnamon, orange, rosewater, strawberry, vanilla

Pectin
low

Ways to preserve
relish, jam, cordial, candied, syrup

How to use
cheese boards, cake filling, to glaze sweet or savoury dishes

Rhubarb shrub

A shrub is a sweet vinegar-based syrup, an American colonial-era take on an English method that used alcohol to preserve fruit, especially berries. The amusing name and fruit used are the only differences between this shrub and raspberry vinegar (see Raspberry vinegar, page 157). The sweet-and-sour syrup makes a thirst-quenching drink when mixed with soda water.

500 g (1 lb 2 oz) rhubarb, washed and dried
200 g (7 oz) sugar, or to taste
150 ml (5 fl oz) apple cider vinegar

1 x 1 litre (1 quart) sterilised jar
1 x 500 ml (1 pint) sterilised bottle

Cut the rhubarb into 5 mm (¼ inch) pieces and layer with the sugar in a sterilised 1 litre (1 quart) glass jar (see page 15). Place the jar in the fridge for 5 days. As the sugar and rhubarb steep, the fruit will release its tart pink juices. Tilt and turn the jar every day to distribute the liquid evenly.

Strain the liquid and pour it into a saucepan. Add the vinegar and bring to the boil, then pour into a warm sterilised 500 ml (1 pint) bottle (see page 15) and seal. Dilute with water to desired taste before drinking and refrigerate after opening.

Mint

Mentha

Plant spring

Harvest winter, spring, summer

Needs cross-pollination no

Pot yes, preferred

Aspect full sun, part shade

Frost tolerant yes

Soil pH 6.5–7.5

This tenacious and hardy perennial herb is seemingly indestructible. Previously I was always happy to let it go without much more nurturing than water. I now pay more attention to its needs with an annual dose of high-nitrogen fertiliser, regular trimming, and dividing plants when pots become congested. Happily, picking mint is the best way to promote new growth. If you have the space, plant a pot each of Apple, Moroccan and Spearmint varieties, and you will always have a ready supply for a delicious mint jelly.

Varieties
Moroccan – dark green leaves with a strong flavour
Apple – hairy, round leaves with a mild, fruity flavour
Spearmint – most common variety of mint with bright green leaves and a mild mint flavour

Nurture
Plant in a pot to avoid runners spreading and taking over. Use free-draining potting mix and water-in well. Keep well watered. Pick leaves regularly to maintain new shoots. Cut plants back and feed with a high-nitrogen fertiliser in autumn to encourage new growth.

Flavour companions
basil, beans, carrot, clove, cucumber, cumin, dill, ginger, lemon, oregano, parsley, potato, thyme, tomato

Pectin
low

Ways to preserve
jelly, vinegar, butter

How to use
on grilled or roast lamb

Mint jelly

Makes about 1½ cups

This jelly is not the lurid green of store-bought varieties. It will, however, deliver an unmistakable mint flavour and provide the quintessential accompaniment to roast lamb. If you must have a vivid green jelly, add a couple of drops of food colouring along with the mint.

1 kg (2 lb 3 oz) Granny Smith apples

400 ml (13½ fl oz) freshly squeezed lemon juice

large bunch of mint, leaves picked

150 g (5½ oz) sugar (approx.)

1 tablespoon apple cider vinegar (approx.)

green food colouring (optional)

2–3 x 150 ml (5 fl oz) sterilised jars

Roughly chop the apples, including the skin and core, and place in a heavy-based saucepan. Add the lemon juice, a handful of mint leaves and 1 litre (1 quart) water. Bring to the boil, then reduce the heat, cover and simmer, stirring occasionally, for 30 minutes or until a soft pulp is formed.

Scoop the mixture into a square of clean muslin sitting in a colander, then gather up the sides and secure with string. Suspend the muslin over a bowl, leaving it to drip overnight. Resist the temptation to squeeze the fruit as this will produce a cloudy jelly.

Place a small saucer in the freezer. Finely chop enough of the remaining mint leaves to yield a good ½ cup.

Measure the extracted liquid in the bowl and return it to a clean saucepan with 150 g (5½ oz) sugar for every 500 ml (1 pint) of the liquid. Cook, stirring, over low heat until the sugar has dissolved. Increase the heat and bring to a rolling boil until a set is achieved – begin testing after 5 minutes. To test, remove the pan from the heat and place a spoonful of jelly on the cold saucer. Pop the saucer back in the freezer for a couple of minutes – if the jelly wrinkles when pushed, it is ready. If not, cook for another 2–3 minutes and test again. When a set is achieved, remove from the heat and stir in the mint and 1 tablespoon of vinegar for every 500 ml (1 pint) of liquid (and food colouring, if using). Pour the jelly into two or three warm sterilised 150 ml (5 fl oz) jars (see page 15), wipe the rims and seal when cold. Refrigerate after opening.

Basil

Ocimum basilicum

Plant seeds in spring, seedlings in early summer

Harvest summer, autumn

Needs cross-pollination no

Pot yes

Aspect sun, part sun

Frost tolerant no

Soil pH 5.5–6.5

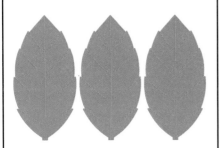

I can't imagine a summer garden without this intensely aromatic herb; an integral flavour in roasted tomato soup (see page 31), a classic pesto, and a beautiful pairing with strawberries. Dollop thawed puree on pizzas or whisk into a vinaigrette.

Varieties
Sweet – classic basil, favoured by cooks
Lettuce Leaf– large, slightly crinkled aromatic leaves
Fino Verde – compact variety, good choice for growing in pots

Nurture
Plant seeds in a tray filled with seed-raising mix and water lightly (basil does not cope well with wet feet). Transfer seedlings to a sunny, sheltered position after the risk of frost has passed, planting into well-drained soil that has been lightly boosted with well-rotted manure or compost. Space seedlings at 30 cm (1 foot) apart. Pinch out tips when seedlings are around 7 cm (2¾ inch) tall and continue to remove tips to encourage bushy growth.

Flavour companions
balsamic vinegar, beans, carrot, clove, garlic, lemon, lime, mint, peach, strawberry, tomato, zucchini

Ways to preserve
puree, frozen

How to use
soups, stews, pizza, pastas

Basil and olive oil puree

Wash the basil leaves, then pat them dry between layers of paper towel and place in a blender. With the blender running on high, gently drip olive oil through the opening in the lid (as if you were making mayonnaise). Go slowly; the aim is to use as little olive oil as possible. Puree until smooth, then spoon into an ice cube tray and freeze. Transfer the frozen blocks to an airtight bag or container and store in the freezer for up to 12 months.

basil leaves
extra virgin olive oil

Tarragon

Artemisia dracunculus

♈ Plant seeds spring

◎ Harvest spring, summer, autumn

❦❦ Needs cross-pollination no

▽ Pot yes

☼ Aspect morning sun and afternoon shade

❄ Frost tolerant yes, plant dies back in winter

⊥ Soil pH 6.5–7.5

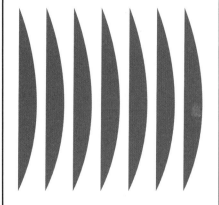

It took me a long time to find the right place for tarragon in my garden. Now that I have a perfect location with morning sun and afternoon shade, I have a vigorous plant with a feathery mass of slender, aromatic leaves. This perennial does not set seed and dies back in winter before bursting back into life in spring. I love tarragon and chicken, and I have developed a habit of freezing small portions of tarragon butter (about 2 teaspoons) that I slip under the breast skin of a chicken before roasting.

Varieties
French – smooth, glossy green leaves, pronounced aniseed flavour
Russian – more robust, but less flavoursome than French variety

Nurture
Take time to find the right position and plant into free-draining, slightly sandy soil. Pinch tips regularly to encourage new growth. Plants will need replacing every 3–4 years.

Flavour companions
asparagus, basil, broad beans, carrot, chicken, dill, mint, parsley, thyme, tomato, zucchini

Ways to preserve
frozen, butter, dried

How to use
sauces, garnish, with fish dishes, on roasted vegetables

Tarragon butter

Makes about ½ cup

You can use this method for a variety of soft-leaf herbs, such as parsley, basil and sage.

Combine all the ingredients in a bowl. Roll into a log, then wrap securely in baking paper and plastic wrap. Store in the freezer, slicing off discs as needed.

125 g (4½ oz) unsalted butter, at room temperature
⅓ cup finely chopped tarragon
1 garlic clove, crushed
1 teaspoon grated lemon zest
1 teaspoon fine salt
½ teaspoon freshly ground pepper

Preserved fruit

Fruit trees were once an integral feature of home gardens. Sadly, this is no longer the case; restraints on time and space, and a belief that growing fruit trees is difficult or time-consuming have seen this tradition fade. The truth is, fruit trees are relatively easy to grow and require little intervention – in my experience, keeping the birds away from the ripening fruit is the most demanding task – and thankfully, there are solutions to the problem of limited space. Espalier trees will grow to occupy vertical space, rather than horizontal, and can soften walls and fences. Multi-graft trees produce more than one variety on a single trunk, removing the need to choose a single fruit when space is limited. Miniature and dwarf varieties are bred for growing in pots, and trees developed to display a columnar habit are ideal for planting in a narrow space along a driveway. If you plan on planting a fruit garden, no matter the size or variety of fruit grown, the best thing you can do is visit a local tree nursery and speak with the experts about the trees best suited to your climate and situation. Of course, there is no need to create a dedicated fruit garden. Look for ways to incorporate a row or two of berry canes along one edge of an existing bed, or to plant miniature or columnar trees as 'pillars' at the corners of beds. The ornamental beauty of citrus trees makes them ideal candidates for use as a feature tree anywhere in the garden.

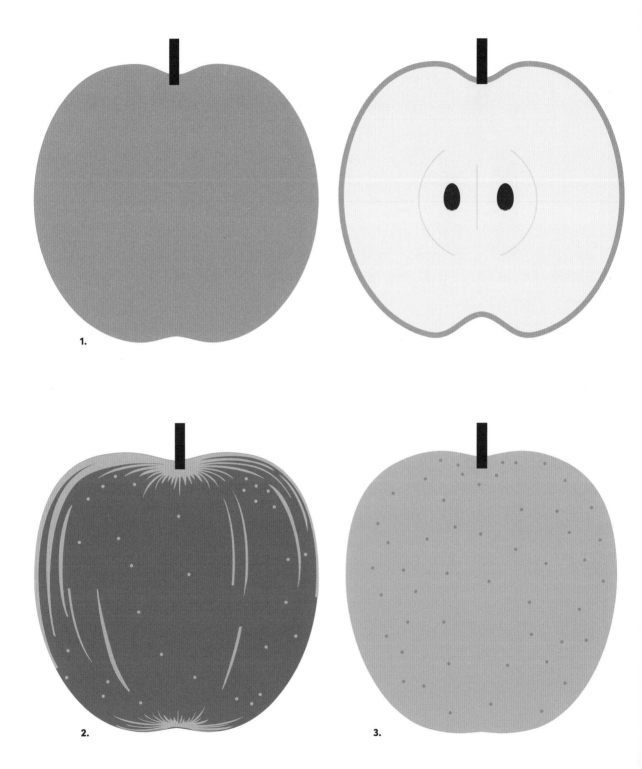

1.

2.

3.

Apples

Malus domestica

It might be an outdated and romantic notion, but I think every garden should have an apple tree or two. Not only do they produce fruit that can be used in a multitude of ways, but the branches, thick with blossom, are such a cheering sight in spring. Most apple varieties need a partner that flowers at the same time to cross-pollinate. Be sure to choose the correct pairing when selecting your trees. Dwarf and miniature varieties are a great solution to limited space, as are multi-grafted apple trees.

♈	**Plant** bareroot in late winter, potted in early spring
◎	**Harvest** late summer, autumn
✂	**Prune** annual, winter
❦	**Needs cross-pollination** yes
☌	**Bears first fruit** third year
⊽	**Pot** yes, miniature and dwarf varieties
☼	**Aspect** full sun
❄	**Frost tolerant** yes
⎏	**Soil pH** 6.5–7.0

Apples

1. Granny Smith
2. Gravenstein
3. Golden Delicious

Varieties
Granny Smith – bright green apples, crisp, not-too-sweet flesh, excellent multi-purpose apple, pollinate with Golden Delicious
Gravenstein – red and yellow fruit with a sweet, tangy flavour; an excellent apple for cooking and preserving, pollinate with early-flowering crabapple
Golden Delicious – produces large quantities of medium-sized fruit that stores well, pollinate with Granny Smith

Nurture
Apples need good drainage and an open situation with good air circulation. Stake when planting. Weed and mulch in spring, water during dry periods and when fruit is forming.

Pectin
unripe, high; ripe, medium

Flavour companions
allspice, apricot, blackberry, cardamom, cherry, cinnamon, clove, cumin, currant, date, ginger, nutmeg, orange, pears, plum, quince, star anise, vanilla

Ways to preserve
bottled, jelly, sauce

How to use
Apple sauce is a classic pairing for roast pork. Bottled pie filling can be used for desserts and breakfast dishes. Jelly can be warmed and used to glaze sweet and savoury dishes.

Apple pie filling

With a jar of this ready-to-go pie filling and frozen pastry sheets, making a delicious apple pie is a doddle.

Peel, quarter and core the apples. Cut the quarters into 2 cm (¾ inch) pieces and toss with the spices, lemon zest and lemon juice.

Place the sugar in a heavy-based saucepan, add 250 ml (1 cup) water and stir over medium heat until the sugar has dissolved. Reduce the heat to low, add the cornflour slurry and stir until the mixture has thickened. Bring to the boil, add the vanilla and apple and stir for a few minutes until the apple is heated through.

Tightly pack the apple mixture into a warm sterilised 1 litre (1 quart) jar (see page 15), allowing 1 cm (½ inch) headspace. Wipe the rims and seal, then process in a water bath for 30 minutes (see page 14).

1 kg (2 lb 3 oz) apples (any variety, or a mixture)
½ teaspoon ground cinnamon
¼ teaspoon freshly grated nutmeg
¼ teaspoon ground allspice
grated zest and juice of ½ lemon
80 g (2¾ oz) sugar
1 tablespoon cornflour (cornstarch) mixed with 1 tablespoon water
1 teaspoon vanilla bean paste

1 x 1 litre (1 quart) sterilised jar

To make an apple pie

Place a baking tray in the oven and preheat to 250°C (500°F).

Line the base of a 23 cm (9 inch) pie dish with readymade shortcrust pastry. Spoon in the apple filling and top with a sheet of puff pastry. Trim and gently seal the edges, then place the pie on the heated baking tray, reduce the oven temperature to 220°C (425°F) and bake for 25 minutes. Reduce the heat to 190°C (375°F) and bake for a further 20–30 minutes until the pastry is golden brown.

Pitted cherries, stoned peaches and blueberries can all be used to prepare a pie filling. Adjust the spices accordingly (see my suggested flavour pairings for each fruit) and process in a water bath for 30 minutes (see page 14).

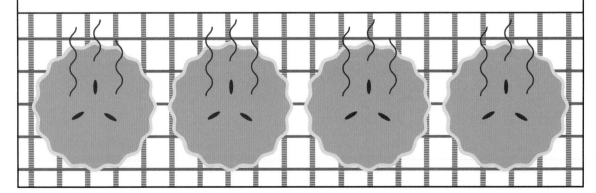

Apple jelly

This jewel-like, delicately flavoured jelly was a pantry staple when I was growing up. It is an easy preserve with a scalable sugar-to-juice ratio, so I have not provided specific quantities here; you can make as little or as much as you like. Cooking the whole apples, including cores and peel, gives a good pectin level which is crucial to the jelly setting. Adding quince increases the setting strength and produces a gloriously pink, perfumed jelly.

apples, washed and drained
quinces (optional)
freshly squeezed lemon juice
    (and any pips; optional)
sugar

Roughly chop the apples, including the seeds and cores, and place in a heavy-based saucepan. Wash the quinces (if using) and wipe with a soft cloth to remove the downy covering, then roughly chop and add to the pan. Add the lemon pips (if you have any; reserve the juice for later) and cover with water. Bring to a gentle boil and cook, stirring occasionally for 30 minutes or until the fruit has softened.

To strain, pour the mixture into a square of clean muslin sitting in a colander, then gather up the sides and secure with string. Suspend the muslin over a bowl, leaving it to drip overnight. Resist the temptation to squeeze the fruit as this will produce a cloudy jelly.

Place a small saucer in the freezer. Measure the extracted liquid in the bowl and return it to a clean saucepan with 1 tablespoon lemon juice and 150 g (5½ oz) sugar for every 250 ml (1 cup) of the liquid. Cook, stirring, over low heat until the sugar has dissolved, then increase the heat and bring to a rolling boil until a set is achieved. To test, remove the pan from the heat and place a spoonful of jelly on the cold saucer. Pop the saucer back in the freezer for a couple of minutes – if the jelly wrinkles when pushed, it is ready. If not, cook for another 5 minutes and test again. Pour the jelly into warm sterilised jars (see page 15), wipe the rims and seal when cold. Refrigerate after opening.

Crabapples

Malus

The pretty blossoms and fragrance of certain crabapple varieties are not the only thing that makes growing these stunning fruit trees so appealing. Their use as pollinators for other trees and the setting qualities of the high-pectin fruit ensure they have an invaluable role in the preserving garden and kitchen.

Plant bareroot in winter, container-grown in late autumn, potted in early spring

Harvest late summer, early autumn

Prune annual, late autumn or winter

Needs cross-pollination no

Bears first fruit second year

Pot yes

Aspect full sun with moist, well-drained soil

Frost tolerant yes

Soil pH 5.5–6.5

Varieties
Eleyi – deep red buds open into purple-pink flowers, makes beautiful apple jelly
Prairie – beautiful variety with white or pink flowers and small red fruit, a valuable cross pollinator for apples

Nurture
Plant bareroot trees (see page 192) into rich, well-drained soil. Stake when planting, add mulch and water generously. Add compost around the roots in spring and a layer of well-rotted manure in autumn. Prune to remove dead or diseased branches and to create an open, airy form.

Flavour companions
allspice, blackberry, cardamom, cinnamon, clove, coriander, cumin, ginger, nutmeg, pear, plum, quince, star anise, vanilla

Pectin
high

Ways to preserve
jam, jelly, pickled

How to use
Jam and jelly are delicious additions to the breakfast table. Jelly and sauces can be used to glaze sweet and savoury dishes, and spiced pickled crabapples are a lovely accompaniment to roast pork. They are also terrific as a source of pectin.

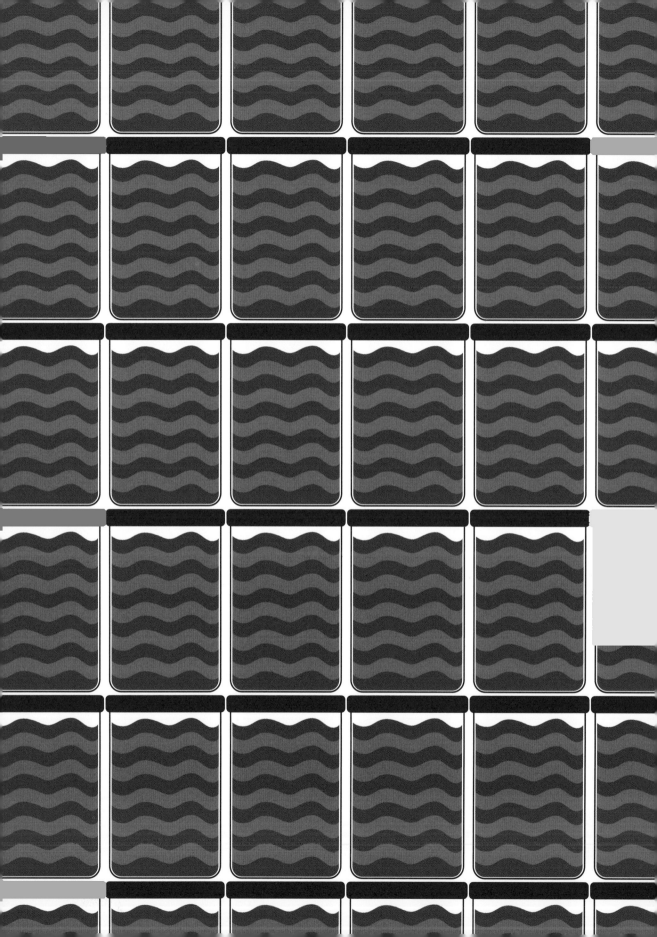

Crabapple jelly

A beautiful, tangy jelly to eat with savoury dishes or on scones with cream. Just like the Apple jelly on page 89, this has a scalable sugar-to-juice ratio, so I have not given specific quantities here.

crabapples
sugar
freshly squeezed lemon juice (optional)

Wash the crabapples and remove the stems. Place in a heavy-based saucepan and add enough water to cover, then bring to a gentle boil and cook for 20–30 minutes until the apples have softened to a pulp.

To strain, pour the apple mixture into a square of clean muslin sitting in a colander, then gather up the sides and secure with string. Suspend the muslin over a bowl, leaving it to drip overnight. Resist the temptation to squeeze the fruit as this will produce a cloudy jelly.

Place a small saucer in the freezer. Measure the extracted liquid in the bowl and return it to a clean saucepan (add in lemon juice, if desired) with 200 g (7 oz) sugar for every 250 ml (1 cup) of the liquid. Cook, stirring, over low heat until the sugar has dissolved, then increase the heat and bring to a rolling boil until a set is achieved. To test, remove the pan from the heat and place a spoonful of jelly on the cold saucer. Pop the saucer back in the freezer for a couple of minutes – if the jelly wrinkles when pushed, it is ready. If not, cook for another 5 minutes and test again. Pour the jelly into warm sterilised jars (see page 15), wipe the rims and seal when cold. Refrigerate after opening.

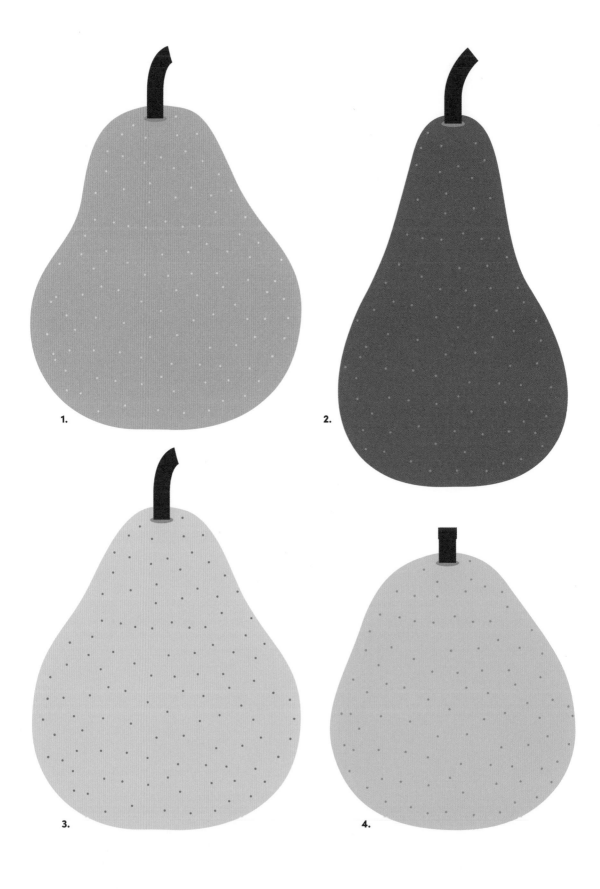

1.

2.

3.

4.

Pears

Pyrus

Stately and enduring, an old pear tree is a beauty to behold. I am always surprised to be reminded of how much I enjoy their subtle, sweet and juicy flavour when I bite into the first pear of the season.

Plant bareroot in late winter; container-grown in late autumn, early spring

Harvest late summer, autumn

Prune annual, winter

Needs cross-pollination yes

Bears first fruit third year

Pot yes, miniature varieties

Aspect sheltered, full sun

Frost tolerant no

Soil pH 6.5

Pears

1. Williams bon Chrétien
2. Beurre Bosc
3. Comice
4. Anjou

Varieties

Williams bon Chrétien – commonly known as a Williams or Bartlett pear; a partly-fertile variety, produces fruit with a smooth, green-yellow skin blushed orange; sweet, and juicy flesh, holds its shape, ideal for bottling, plant with Beurre Bosc or Comice nearby

Beurre Bosc – medium tree with an upright habit; produces long, brown fruit with creamy flesh, suitable for bottling and butter, pollinate with any other pear

Comice – semi-dwarf compact tree, French variety, sweet and juicy, range from small to large in size, red or green fruit

Anjou – squat, bright green fruit ripens from the inside out, holds shape when cooked, good for bottling

Nurture

Plant into well-drained soil that has been enriched to a level of 50–60 cm (1½–2 feet). Water during dry periods and when the fruit begins to swell. Apply a high-potash fertiliser in early spring after the first year. Weed and apply mulch in spring. Flowers appear in early to mid-spring and are at risk of frost damage during this time.

Flavour companions

allspice, apple, apricot, basil, blackberry, blueberry, cardamom, cherry, chocolate, cinnamon, clove, date, ginger, lemon, mace, mint, nutmeg, orange, passionfruit, quince, raspberry, rhubarb, star anise, strawberry, vanilla, walnut

Pectin

low

Ways to preserve

bottled, butter, chutney

How to use

Pear butter spread on a crumpet is a delicious and delicate alternative to honey. Great in pies, cakes and crumbles or mixed through yoghurt.

Autumn chutney

This chutney is a lovely way to celebrate the arrival of autumn pears and use the last of summer's tomatoes. If there is a lag between tomatoes and pears, freeze whole tomatoes and add them to the pan, still frozen, when you have pears available.

Peel and core apples and pears, then cut into rough 2 cm (¾ inch) dice. Peel the tomatoes (see page 16), remove the seeds and cut into rough 2 cm (¾ inch) dice. Place the apple, pear and tomato in a heavy-based saucepan and add the remaining ingredients. Bring to the boil, then reduce the heat and simmer for 1½ hours, stirring occasionally at first and more frequently towards the end.

Ladle the mixture into four or five warm sterilised 200 ml (7 fl oz) jars (see page 15). Wipe the rims and seal when cold. Leave the chutney in a cool, dark place for 4 weeks before using, then refrigerate after opening.

1 kg (2 lb 3 oz) Granny Smith apples
500 g (1 lb 2 oz) pears
700 g (1 lb 9 oz) ripe tomatoes
1 kg (2 lb 3 oz) brown sugar
125 g (4½ oz) sultanas (golden raisins)
125 g (4½ oz) raisins
600 ml (1¼ pints) white wine vinegar
½ teaspoon ground mace
½ teaspoon cayenne pepper
½ teaspoon ground cloves
½ teaspoon ground ginger
1 teaspoon yellow mustard seeds

4–5 x 200 ml (7 fl oz) sterilised jars

Pear butter

This delicious puree can be stirred through yoghurt, spread on toast or used as a filling in biscuits or cakes. Don't limit yourself to the spices I have suggested here – star anise, ginger and lemon are all great with pear, so use what you like.

Peel and core the pears and cut them into even-sized chunks. Place in a heavy-based saucepan, add the orange zest and juice and bring to the boil, then reduce the heat and simmer, covered, for 30–40 minutes until softened.

Pass the pear mixture through the fine disc of a food mill and place in a clean heavy-based saucepan. Stir in the remaining ingredients. Cook over low heat, stirring regularly, for 30–40 minutes until the mixture has thickened and a spatula dragged through leaves a clear trail.

Spoon the pear butter into two warm sterilised 200 ml (7 fl oz) jars (see page 15), leaving 1 cm (½ inch) headspace. Wipe the rims, seal the jars and process in a water bath for 15 minutes (see page 14). Refrigerate after opening.

800 g (1 lb 12 oz) pears
grated zest and juice of ½ orange
¼ teaspoon ground cinnamon
1 teaspoon brown sugar
½ vanilla bean, split and seeds scraped

2 x 200 ml (7 fl oz) sterilised jars

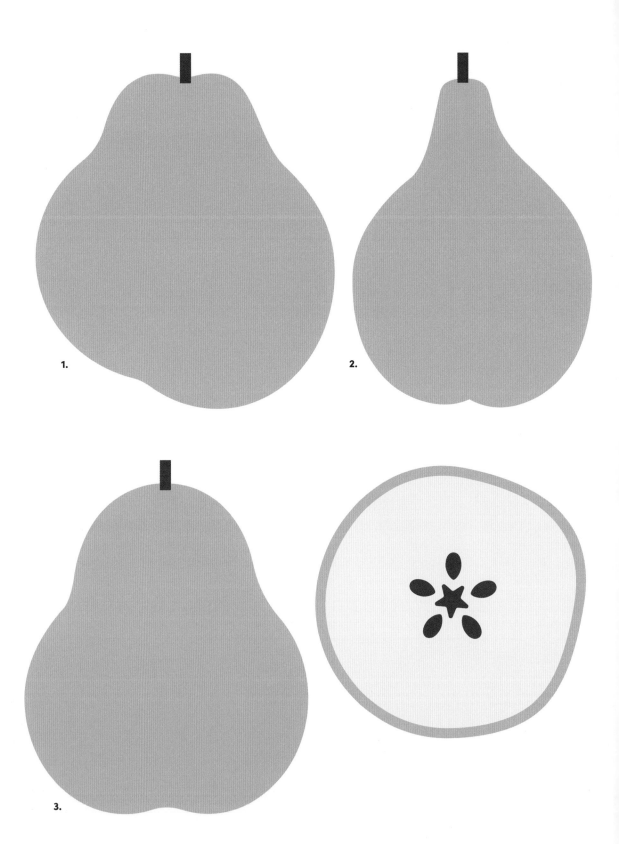

1.

2.

3.

Quince

Cydonia oblonga

This medium-sized tree has ornamental and productive appeal with beautiful blossoms and delicious fruit – often twice a year. I love the bumpy, down-covered form of the fruit and the incredible rose-like perfume that fills the room when I place a bowl filled with this ancient fruit in the kitchen.

Plant bareroot and container-grown in winter

Harvest autumn

Prune annual, late autumn to early spring

Needs cross-pollination no

Bears first fruit third year

Pot yes

Aspect warm, well-drained situation

Frost tolerant late frosts will damage flowers

Soil pH 5.0–7.0

Varieties
Fuller's – large, bright yellow fruit, pear-shaped with smooth flesh that turns pale pink when cooked
Smyrna – long yellow fruit, self-pollinating but will produce more fruit with cross-pollination; excellent all-round variety for jams, jellies, stewing, poaching, roasting and paste
Champion – hardy, heavy-cropping variety with multiple uses

Nurture
Plant into soil that has been deeply dug through with the well-rotted manure or compost. Mulch well after planting and apply pellet fertiliser in late winter. Water during dry spells. Look for any suckers that emerge at the base of the tree and remove them at ground level. Lightly prune annually to form the shape. Fruit grows on the season's new wood growth, so it is important to remove old growth.

Flavour companions
allspice, apple, cinnamon, clove, ginger, honey, lemon, orange, vanilla

Pectin
high

Ways to preserve
jam, jelly, paste, chutney

How to use
cheese boards

Quince

1. Fuller's
2. Smyrna
3. Champion

Quince jelly

Makes about 2 cups

This recipe produces the most beautiful pinkish-orange jelly with an unmistakable perfume. It is delicious eaten with cheese and can be used as the basis of a glaze for both sweet and savoury dishes. The quantities here are scalable, making this a rewarding and unfussy way to deal with this most glorious fruit.

1 kg (2 lb 2 oz) quinces
400 g (14 oz) sugar (approx.)
60 ml (¼ cup) freshly squeezed lemon juice (approx.)

2–3 200 ml (7 fl oz) sterilised jars

Wash the quinces and wipe with a soft cloth to remove any downy covering, then roughly chop. Place the chopped quince, seeds and cores in a heavy-based saucepan and add 1 litre (1 quart) water. Cover and cook over medium heat, stirring occasionally, until the fruit has softened and collapsed – this can take as long as 1 hour, but keep an eye on it.

To strain, pour the mixture into a square of clean muslin sitting in a colander, then gather up the sides and secure with string. Suspend the muslin over a bowl, leaving it to drip overnight. Resist the temptation to squeeze the fruit as this will produce a cloudy jelly.

Place a small saucer in the freezer. Measure the extracted liquid in the bowl and return it to a clean saucepan with 200g (7 oz) sugar and 60 ml (¼ cup) lemon juice for every 250 ml (1 cup) of the liquid. Cook, stirring, over low heat until the sugar has dissolved, then increase the heat and bring to a rolling boil until a set is achieved. To test, remove the pan from the heat and place a spoonful of jelly on the cold saucer. Pop the saucer back in the freezer for a couple of minutes – if the jelly wrinkles when pushed, it is ready. If not, cook for another 5 minutes and test again. Pour the jelly into warm sterilised jars (see page 15), wipe the rims and seal when cold. Refrigerate after opening.

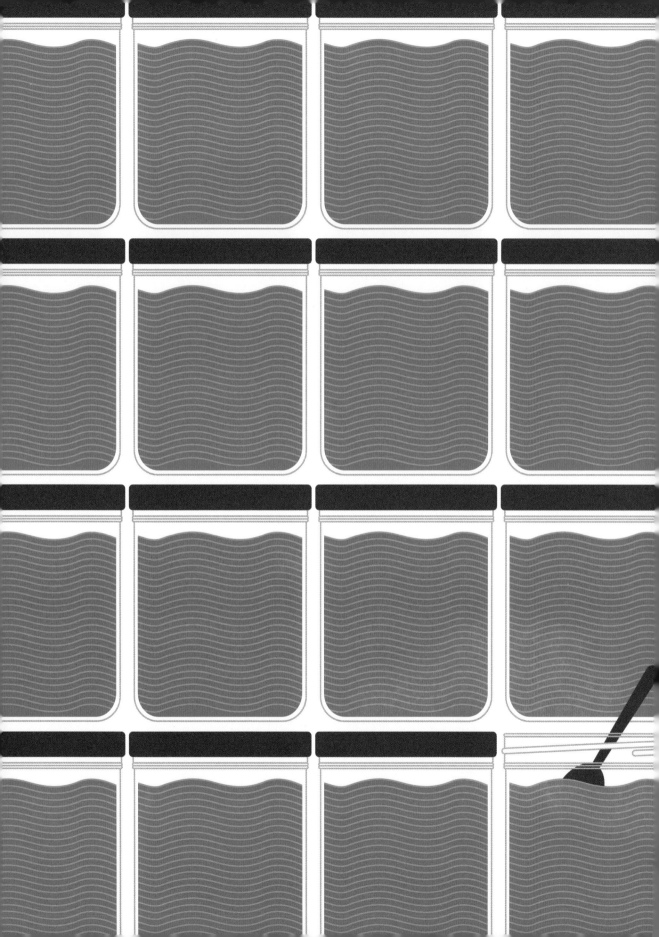

1.

2.

3.

Oranges

Citrus sinensis

Orange trees are incredibly handsome; glossy, dark green leaves, sweetly scented blossoms, and a compact canopy dotted with brightly coloured orbs put them centre stage in any garden.

Plant spring

Harvest *Seville* – winter, spring
Navel – autumn, winter, spring
Valencia – spring, summer

Prune lightly after harvest

Needs cross-pollination no

Bears first fruit third year

Pot yes

Aspect sun

Frost tolerant yes

Soil pH 6.0–6.5

Varieties
Navel – seedless, round, thick-skinned fruit with distinctive indentation at one end, good flavour in jelly
Seville – smooth-skinned with bitter flesh, high pectin content, classic marmalade fruit
Valencia – thin-skinned fruit harvested in spring and summer, sweet and fast growing, good for marmalade, ideal for juicing

Nurture
Plant into well-drained soil with well-rotted manure or compost, dug into a depth of 30 cm (1 foot). Choose a sheltered position, apply a layer of mulch after planting and water well during dry periods. Fertilise with a complete fertiliser in spring. Thin fruit of a heavy crop to prevent branches breaking.

Flavour companions
apple, apricot, basil, blackberry, blueberry, cardamom, cherry, cinnamon, clove, coriander, cumin, cumquat, date, fennel, fig, ginger, grape, grapefruit, lemon, lime, mint, nutmeg, paprika, parsley, passionfruit, peach, pear, plum, quince, raspberry, rhubarb, saffron, star anise, strawberry, thyme, tomato, walnut

Pectin
moderate–high

Ways to preserve
jelly, marmalade, cordial, dried, syrup

How to use
cakes, puddings, salads

Oranges

1. Navel
2. Seville
3. Valencia

Orange jelly

Makes about 2 cups

This sunshine-orange jelly is my spread of choice on hot buttered crumpets.

juice of 1.5 kg (3 lb 5 oz) oranges
juice of 2 large lemons
25 g (1 oz) powdered pectin
250 g (9 oz) sugar

2–3 x 200 ml (7 fl oz) sterilised jars

Combine the juices and pectin in a heavy-based saucepan and bring to the boil, stirring constantly. When the juice is boiling, add the sugar and simmer, stirring, until the sugar has dissolved. Use a spoon to skim off any white foam.

Pour the jelly into two or three warm sterilised 200 ml (7 fl oz) jars (see page 15). Wipe the rims and seal when cold. Refrigerate after opening.

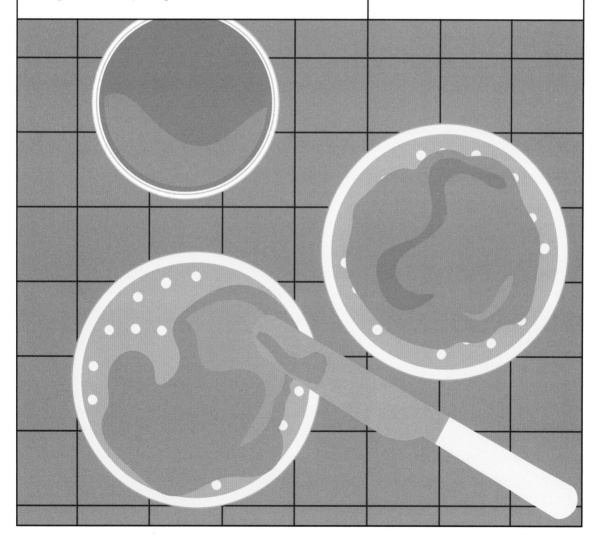

Grapefruit

Citrus paradisi

Grapefruit is another striking ornamental tree with clusters of large fruits. I love the distinctive flavour of this sweet, tart and bitter fruit. It is a natural choice for zesty marmalade but also makes a lovely jelly (see Orange jelly page 105) and a refreshing cordial (see Lemon squash page 113).

Plant autumn, winter, spring

Harvest autumn, winter

Prune annual, late winter or early spring

Needs cross-pollination no

Bears first fruit second year

Pot yes, dwarf or miniature varieties

Aspect open, sunny position

Frost tolerant yes

Soil pH 6.6–7.3

Varieties
Wheeny – thick-skinned and sour fruit with pale yellow flesh
Marsh Seedless – vigorous, productive trees with very sweet and juicy fruit, seedless
Star Ruby – medium-sized, red-fleshed fruit with smooth, thin peel

Nurture
Plant into well-drained soil, mulch in spring, and fertilise in spring and summer. Water deeply during dry spells. Thin fruit of a heavy crop to prevent damage to branches. Prune when needed to maintain size and shape and remove any dead, damaged or diseased branches.

Flavour companions
basil, ginger, lemon, lime, mint, orange, raspberry, rosemary, star anise, strawberry, tarragon, thyme

Pectin
high

Ways to preserve
marmalade, jelly, cordial, dried, dehydrated

How to use
glaze for sweet and savoury dishes, in steamed pudding, paired with soft cheeses

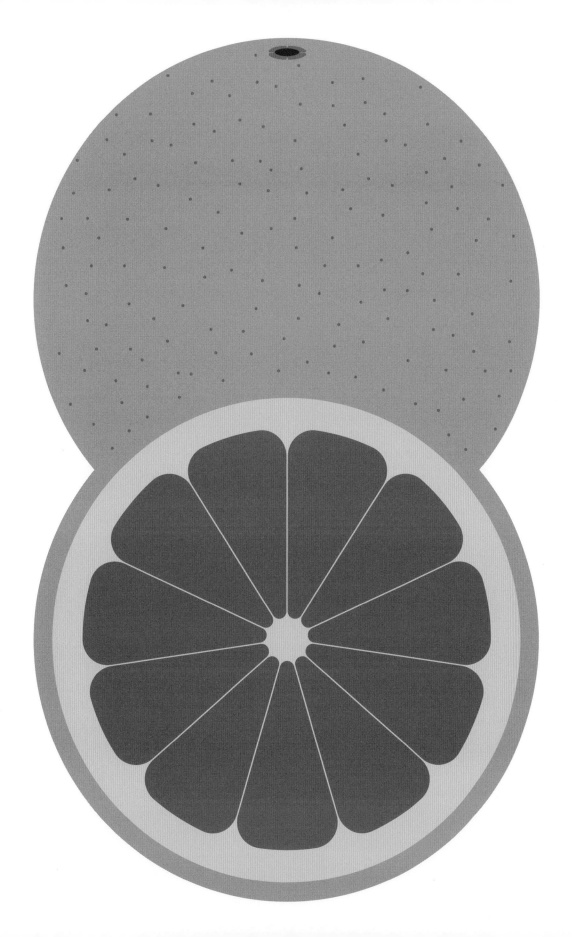

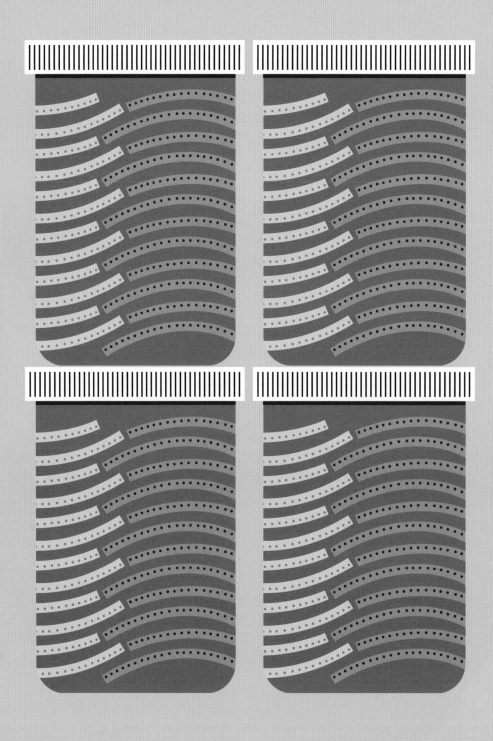

Grapefruit marmalade

Makes about 4 cups

You need to start this recipe a day ahead. The peel has to be soaked for 24 hours to allow it to soften and avoid a 'chewy' or 'tough' marmalade.

1 kg (2 lb 3 oz) grapefruit, washed
   and dried
400 g (14 oz) lemons, washed and dried
2.5 kg (5½ lb) sugar (approx.)

4–5 x 200 ml (7 fl oz) sterilised jars

Peel the grapefruit and lemons, then cut the peel into fine strips, removing and reserving the pith. Cover the sliced peel with water and leave to soak for 24 hours. Drain.

Juice the grapefruit and lemons, reserving the pips. Store the juice in the fridge while the peel is soaking.

Tie the reserved pips and pith in a muslin bag and place in a heavy-based saucepan. Add the juice, soaked peel and 2.5 litres (2½ quarts) water. Bring to the boil, then reduce the heat and simmer, covered, for 1 hour or until the peel is very soft.

Place a small saucer in the freezer. Use the back of a spoon to gently press the muslin bag against the side of the pan, squeezing out more pectin, then discard the bag. Measure the grapefruit mixture and allow 200 g (7 oz) sugar for every 250 ml (1 cup) of the fruit. Return the fruit to the pan and add the sugar. Cook, stirring, over low heat until the sugar has dissolved, then increase the heat and bring to a rolling boil. Cook without stirring until a set is achieved. Start testing after 10–15 minutes. To do this, remove the pan from the heat and place a spoonful of marmalade on the cold saucer. Pop the saucer back in the freezer for a couple of minutes – if the marmalade wrinkles when pushed, it is ready. If not, cook for another 5 minutes and test again.

When the marmalade is at setting point, turn off the heat and allow it to sit for 5 minutes, then pour it into four or five warm sterilised 200 ml (7 fl oz) jars (see page 15). Wipe the rims and seal when cold. Refrigerate after opening.

Lemons

Citrus limon

A lemon tree is often the first choice for the home fruit garden. Relatively easy to grow, suitable for pots, and fruiting for long periods – lemons are essential in the preserving pantry. I always feel discombobulated when I don't have a ready supply, and it does happen for a period of each year. Growing more than one variety can shorten the length of this 'lemon drought'.

Plant spring

Harvest autumn, winter, spring

Prune annual, not during flowering and harvesting season

Needs cross-pollination no

Bears first fruit second year

Pot yes, miniature and dwarf varieties

Aspect full sun

Frost tolerant depends on variety (Eureka, no; Meyer and Seville, yes)

Soil pH 6.6–7.3

Lemons

1. Eureka
2. Meyer
3. Lisbon

Varieties
Eureka – thick-skinned with acidic flesh, generally thornless and seedless, not frost tolerant
Meyer – small and juicy fruit with smooth, thin skin, sweeter than other lemons, best for cordial, good for candied peel, frost tolerant
Lisbon – smooth-skinned, high acidity, excellent multi-use variety, frost tolerant

Nurture
Plant into well-drained soil, mulch in spring and fertilise in spring and summer. Water deeply during dry spells. As roots are close to the surface, take care not to disturb the soil. Prune when needed to maintain size and shape and remove any dead, damaged or diseased branches.

Flavour companions
apple, apricot, basil, bay leaf, blackberry, blueberry, cardamom, cayenne, cherry, cinnamon, date, ginger, gooseberry, grape, grapefruit, lime, mint, orange, oregano, parsley, passionfruit, peach, pear, plum, poppy seed, quince, raspberry, rhubarb, sage, thyme, vanilla

Pectin
high

Ways to preserve
marmalade, cordial, candied, frozen, cured in jars, paste, butter, pickled, dried

How to use
salsas, chimichurri, salads, stews, marinades, pastas, desserts, vinaigrette, with roasted vegetables, on fish

1.

2.

3.

Lemon squash

Makes about 4 cups

I don't think I have ever been without a bottle of this cordial in the fridge. When I was growing up we would take a large cooler full on every picnic or trip to the beach – mixed with carbonated water and a dash of bitters it makes a delicious thirst quencher. I have tweaked my mum's original recipe, cutting down the sugar (it's still sweet, but remember the syrup is diluted before drinking) and increased the quantity of lemon to give it extra zing. You can also use this recipe with oranges, limes, grapefruit or a mixture of citrus fruit.

grated zest and juice of 5 lemons
440 g (2 cups) sugar
500 ml (1 pint) boiling water
1 teaspoon tartaric acid

2 x 500 ml (1 pint) sterilised bottles

Combine the lemon zest and juice with the sugar in a large heatproof bowl. Pour over the boiling water and stir until the sugar has dissolved. Stir in the tartaric acid, then leave to steep for 2–3 hours.

Strain the mixture into a saucepan and bring to the boil, then pour into two warm sterilised 500 ml (1 pint) bottles (see page 15). Dilute before drinking and refrigerate after opening.

Limes

Citrus latifolia (Tahitian lime/Persian lime)
Citrus aurantifolia (Key lime/West Indian lime)

A lime tree is an excellent investment in the preserving garden. Not only do the trees create a focal point, but their long fruit-bearing season offers a ready supply that extends well beyond their commercial availability.

Plant spring

Harvest autumn, winter, spring

Prune late winter, early spring when needed

Needs cross-pollination no

Bears first fruit first year

Pot yes

Aspect full sun to partial shade

Frost tolerant no

Soil pH 6.6–7.3

Varieties
Tahitian lime (Persian) – vivid green skin turns yellow as the fruit ripens, best picked when green, produces fruit across 6 months in the right conditions
Key lime (West Indian) – small fruit with intense lime flavour, fruit is ripe when skin is yellow, great for marmalade

Nurture
Plant into well-drained soil, mulch in spring and fertilise in spring and summer. Water daily during dry spells and deeply at least once or twice a week – lime trees need consistent moisture in their soil to grow well. Around 6–8 hours per day of bright sunlight is ideal.

Flavour companions
apple, apricot, coconut, coriander, ginger, gooseberry, grapefruit, lemon, mint, orange, passionfruit, plum, raspberry, strawberry, tomato

Pectin
high

Ways to preserve
marmalade, cordial, candied, frozen, dehydrated, dried, fermented, paste, butter

How to use
baking, vinaigrettes, marinades, mixed through Greek yoghurt, in margaritas

Limes

1. Tahitian lime (Persian)
2. Key lime (West Indian)

1.

2.

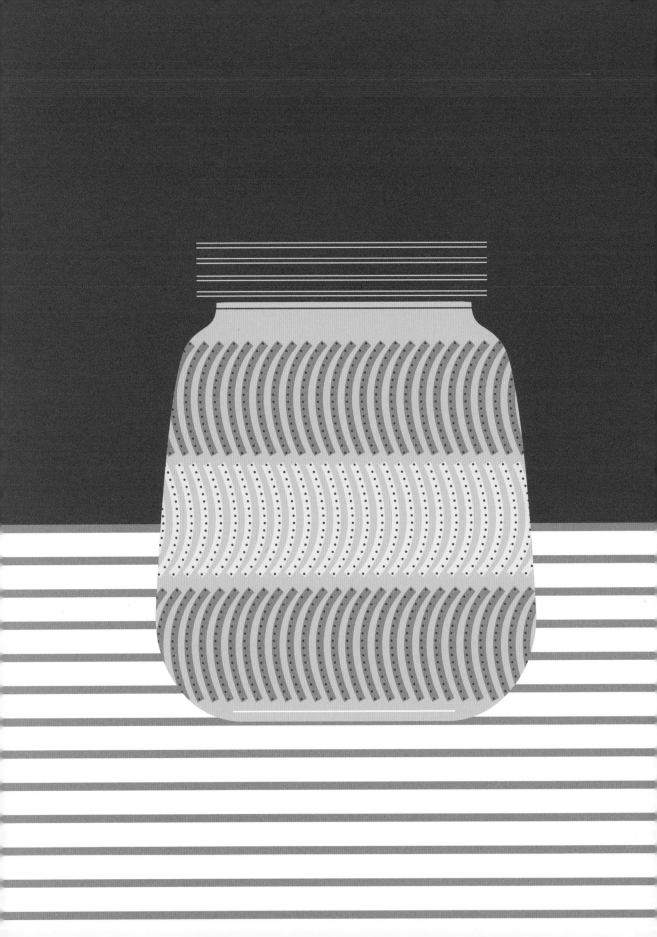

Lime and lemon marmalade

Makes about 4 cups

A sure-fire way to put a little pep in your morning, this zesty breakfast spread also makes a delicious steamed pudding: mix 3 tablespoons of marmalade with 1 tablespoon of lemon or lime juice and place in the base of a pudding basin before filling with batter. Choose limes that are barely ripe or slightly under-ripe to ensure an intense lime flavour and high pectin content.

300 g (10½ oz) limes, washed and dried
200 g (7 oz) lemons, washed and dried
600 g (1 lb 5 oz) sugar (approx.)

4–5 x 200 ml (7 fl oz) sterilised jars

Peel the limes and lemons, then cut the peel into fine strips, removing and reserving the pith. Roughly chop the flesh, reserving the pips as you go.

Tie the reserved pips and pith in a muslin bag and place in a heavy-based saucepan. Add the peel, flesh and 1 litre (1 quart) water. Bring to the boil, then reduce the heat and simmer, covered, for 1 hour or until the peel is very soft.

Place a small saucer in the freezer. Discard the muslin bag of pips and pith. Measure the citrus mixture and allow 150 g (5½ oz) sugar for every 250 ml (1 cup) of the fruit. Return the fruit to a clean saucepan and add the sugar. Cook, stirring, over low heat until the sugar has dissolved, then increase the heat and bring to a rolling boil. Cook without stirring until a set is achieved. Start testing for set after 15–20 minutes. To do this, remove the pan from the heat and place a spoonful of marmalade on the cold saucer. Pop the saucer back in the freezer for a couple of minutes – if the marmalade wrinkles when pushed, it is ready. If not, cook for another 5 minutes and test again.

When the marmalade is at setting point, turn off the heat and allow it to sit for 5 minutes, then pour it into four or five warm sterilised 200 ml (7 fl oz) jars (see page 15). Wipe the rims and seal when cold. Refrigerate after opening

Apricots

Prunus armeniaca

I love all stone fruits, but apricots are my stand-out favourite. With perfumed flesh and orange skin blushed crimson, tree-ripened, homegrown apricots offer the perfect balance of tang and sweetness. Their season is never long enough and the harvest never large enough as I bake them in crumbles, use them as the main ingredient in savoury chutney, or cook up big batches of jam to spread on sourdough toast.

Plant bareroot in late winter, potted in early spring

Harvest summer

Prune annual, summer

Needs cross-pollination no

Bears first fruit second year

Pot yes, miniature and dwarf varieties

Aspect full sun

Frost tolerant no

Soil pH 6.0–7.0

Apricots

1. Tilton
2. Moorpark
3. Glengarry

Varieties
Tilton – medium-sized, self-pollinating, sweet and juicy, heart-shaped fruit, ideal for bottling and jam making, early-fruiting and resistant to late frosts
Moorpark – deep orange flesh with a rich, sweet flavour
Glengarry – large crops of small, pale golden fruit

Nurture
Prepare a well-drained, rich, loamy soil. Soak roots and prune branches of bareroot trees (see page 192) before planting. Weed around the trunk and apply mulch in spring (keeping away from the trunk). Water regularly while tree is establishing, and during dry spells to ensure sweet, juicy fruit. Prune in early autumn immediately after fruiting to encourage healing and reduce risk of disease. Potted trees should be watered with a weak solution of liquid fertiliser before they are planted into a hole that is twice as wide and one and a half times as deep as the pot.

Flavour companions
apple, blackberry, blueberry, cardamom, cherry, cinnamon, ginger, lemon, nutmeg, orange, peach, plum, raspberry, saffron, strawberries, vanilla

Pectin
moderate

Ways to preserve
chutney, jam, bottled, dried

How to use
Add a teaspoon of apricot chutney into coleslaw dressing. Apricot jam can be warmed and used to glaze a fruit tart. Great in crumbles, cobblers and cakes.

1.

2.

3.

Apricot jam

I like thick apricot jam packed with flavour so I cut the fruit into small pieces. If you prefer jam with large chunks of fruit that have held their shape, simply halve the apricots.

Place a small saucer in the freezer. Cut the apricots in half and remove the stones, then roughly cut the flesh into 2 cm (¾ inch) cubes. Place the fruit and lemon juice in a heavy-based saucepan, add 400 ml (13½ fl oz) water and bring to the boil over medium heat. Cover and simmer, stirring occasionally, for 15 minutes or until the apricot has softened. Reduce the heat, add the sugar and stir gently until it has dissolved – if you like a chunky jam, take care not to break up the fruit too much. Bring the mixture to a rolling boil and cook for 15 minutes or until a set is achieved. To test, remove the pan from the heat and place a spoonful of jam on the cold saucer. Pop the saucer back in the freezer for a couple of minutes – if the jam wrinkles when pushed, it is ready. If not, cook for another 5 minutes and test again.

Pour the jam into three or four warm sterilised 200 ml (7 fl oz) jars (see page 15), wipe the rims and seal when cold. Refrigerate after opening.

1 kg (2 lb 3 oz) just-ripe apricots, washed and dried

2 tablespoons freshly squeezed lemon juice

750 g (1 lb 11 oz) sugar

3–4 x 200 ml (7 fl oz) sterilised jars

Apricot chutney

Makes about 3 cups

Like all chutneys, this spicy-sweet mixture improves with age and makes a lovely gift. It's particularly good stirred through mayonnaise with some garam masala to make a dressing for coleslaw.

Cut the apricots in half and remove the stones, then chop the flesh into 1 cm (½ inch) pieces.

Tie the cloves, allspice and peppercorns in a small square of muslin. Place in a heavy-based saucepan with all the remaining ingredients, except the salt, and bring to the boil over medium heat. Reduce the heat to low and simmer, stirring occasionally, for 2 hours or until the mixture has thickened, reduced in volume and darkened in colour. Keep a close eye on it during the last hour, stirring more frequently so it doesn't catch on the base of the pan. Add the salt and bring the mixture back to the boil, stirring to prevent burning.

Remove the pan from the heat. Ladle the chutney into three or four warm sterilised 200 ml (7 fl oz) jars (see page 15). Wipe the rims and seal when cool. Refrigerate after opening.

3 kg (6 lb 10 oz) apricots, washed and dried
1 tablespoon whole cloves
1 tablespoon whole allspice
1 tablespoon whole black peppercorns
4 large onions, cut into 1 cm (½ inch) dice
900 g (2 lb) sugar
1 litre (1 quart) brown malt vinegar
8 garlic cloves, chopped
2 tablespoons ground ginger
60 g (¼ cup) fine salt

3–4 x 200 ml (7 fl oz) sterilised jars

Peaches

Prunus persica

When choosing a peach tree with the intention of bottling fruit, look for a yellow-flesh, freestone variety. Yellow peaches retain their shape well during processing, and the pit of a freestone peach comes away from the flesh easily. A clingstone requires you to prise the pit from the flesh with a small knife or peach pitter – a messy, slippery process. If the fruit is going to be cooked down when making a relish or jam, then the choice of freestone or clingstone peaches is less critical.

♀	**Plant** bareroot in late winter, potted in early spring
◎	**Harvest** summer
✂	**Prune** annual, late winter before blossoming
🐝	**Needs cross-pollination** no
♂	**Bears first fruit** second year
🗑	**Pot** yes, miniature and dwarf varieties
☼	**Aspect** full sun
✳	**Frost tolerant** partially, will not endure frost when pits are developing
⏚	**Soil pH** 6.5–7.0

Varieties

Blackburn Elberta – freestone, large with yellow flesh, great for bottling

Bulida – large, firm, very sweet fruit, dwarf tree variety

Nurture

Prepare soil so that it is rich, loamy and well-drained. Soak roots and prune branches of bareroot trees (see page 192) before planting. Water regularly while tree is establishing and during dry periods. Weed around the trunk, mulch and feed annually in late winter with an all-purpose fertiliser. Water potted trees with a weak solution of liquid fertiliser before planting into a hole twice as wide and one and a half times as deep as the pot in which it was growing, filling the bottom of the hole with worked soil to ensure the tree sits at the same level in the ground as it did in the pot.

Flavour companions

allspice, almond, apple, apricot, basil, bay leaf, blackberry, blueberry, cherry, cinnamon, clove, ginger, lemon, lime, mace, mint, nutmeg, orange, passionfruit, pineapple, plum, raspberry, saffron, star anise, strawberry, tarragon, vanilla

Pectin

low

Ways to preserve

bottled, jam, chutney, dried

How to use

Bottled peaches are a versatile pantry staple: topped with crumble and baked for a quick dessert, sliced on top of yoghurt and granola, in a salsa, or added to a salad along with a salty cheese such as fetta.

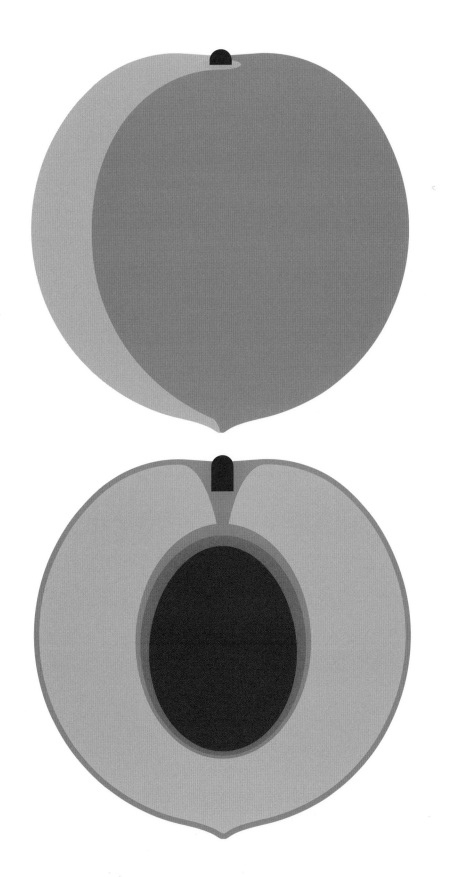

Peach salsa

Makes about 4 cups

This salsa balances the sweetness of peaches with the heat of jalapeño and cayenne. It's delicious with fish and chicken, stirred through steamed broccoli, and an essential side at any barbecue.

Cut the peaches, tomatoes and pineapple into 1–2 cm (½–¾ inch) dice. Place in a heavy-based saucepan, add the remaining ingredients and bring to the boil, stirring occasionally. Cook at a gentle boil, stirring every now and then, for 10–15 minutes until the salsa has thickened slightly.

Pour the hot salsa into four or five warm sterilised 200 ml (7 fl oz) jars (see page 15), leaving 1 cm (½ inch) headspace. Gently tap the jars on the countertop to help the contents settle, then wipe the rims and seal the jars. Process in a water bath for 10 minutes (see page 14). Leave to sit in a cool dark place for 4 weeks before using. Refrigerate after opening.

1 kg (2 lb 3 oz) peaches, peeled (see page 16), halved, stones removed

300 g (10½ oz) tomatoes, peeled (see page 16), seeds removed

½ pineapple, peeled and cored

1 red onion, finely diced

1 red capsicum (pepper), seeds removed, finely diced

2 jalapeño peppers (red or green), seeds removed, very finely chopped

2 garlic cloves, minced

55 g (¼ cup) brown sugar

2 teaspoons ground cumin

1 teaspoon cayenne pepper

1 teaspoon fine salt

¼ teaspoon ground coriander

125 ml (½ cup) white vinegar

4–5 x 200 ml (7 fl oz) sterilised jars

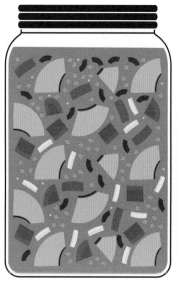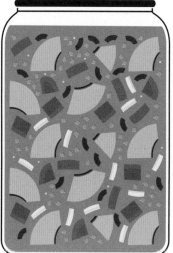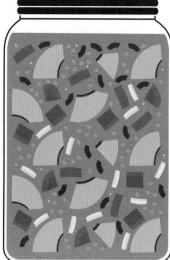

Peach and ginger jam

Makes about 4 cups

Peach and ginger make an excellent pairing – a mingling of sweetness and subtle, spicy warmth.

....

Cut the peaches in half, remove the stones and chop into rough 2.5 cm (1 inch) dice. Peel, core and chop the apples into similar-sized pieces.

Place a small saucer in the freezer. Combine the peach, apple, ginger, lemon zest and juice in a heavy-based saucepan and bring to the boil over medium heat. Reduce the heat to low and cook, covered, for 30 minutes or until the fruit has softened. Still over low heat, add the sugar and cook, stirring, without letting the mixture boil until the sugar has dissolved. Bring to the boil, remove the lid and cook for another 15–20 minutes until a set is achieved. To test, remove the pan from the heat and place a spoonful of jam on the cold saucer. Pop the saucer back in the freezer for a couple of minutes – if the jam wrinkles when pushed, it is ready. If not, cook for another 5 minutes and test again.

Pour the jam into four or five warm sterilised 200 ml (7 fl oz) jars (see page 15), wipe the rims and seal when cold.

1 kg (2 lb 3 oz) peaches, peeled (see page 16)
2 apples
1 tablespoon freshly grated ginger
1½ teaspoons grated lemon zest
125 ml (½ cup) freshly squeezed lemon juice
1 kg (2 lb 3 oz) sugar

4–5 x 200 ml (7 fl oz) sterilised jars

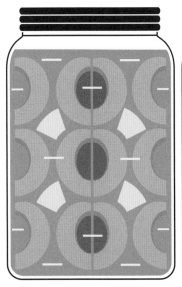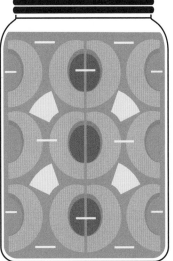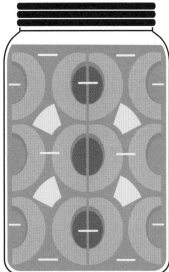

Plums

Prunus domestica

Masses of early blossom in shades of pink, purple and red are a sure sign of the changing season, and, to my mind, enough reason to have plum trees in the garden. With a multitude of varieties and forms to choose from it is easy to have a ready supply of this versatile fruit.

Plant bareroot in late autumn, late winter; container-grown in late autumn, early spring

Harvest summer, autumn

Prune annual, summer, after fruiting

Needs cross-pollination depends on variety

Bears first fruit third year

Pot yes, miniature and dwarf varieties

Aspect full sun

Frost tolerant partially, will not endure frost when flowering (early to mid-spring)

Soil pH 6.0–6.5

Plums

1. Greengage
2. Mariposa
3. Damson

Varieties

Greengage – smallish, round fruit with green-yellow skin and dark yellow flesh, harvest in late summer for jam and bottling

Mariposa – summer fruiting blood plum with sweet, juicy flesh, delicious eaten fresh, produces gorgeous dark red jams and sauces

Damson – small purplish fruit with yellow flesh, good for jam

Nurture

Plant in a sheltered, full-sun position into well-drained soil that has been boosted with the addition of compost to 60 cm (2 feet). Stake when planting. Apply a complete fertiliser annually in late winter and mulch each year in early spring. Water well during dry periods and while fruiting.

Flavour companions

allspice, almond, apricot, bay leaf, cherry, cinnamon, clove, coriander, ginger, lemon, mace, nectarine, nutmeg, orange, peach, raspberry, star anise, strawberry, vanilla

Pectin

moderate

Ways to preserve

jam, sauce, chutney, bottled, frozen

How to use

marinades, as a glaze, in cakes and puddings, paired with a soft goat's cheese

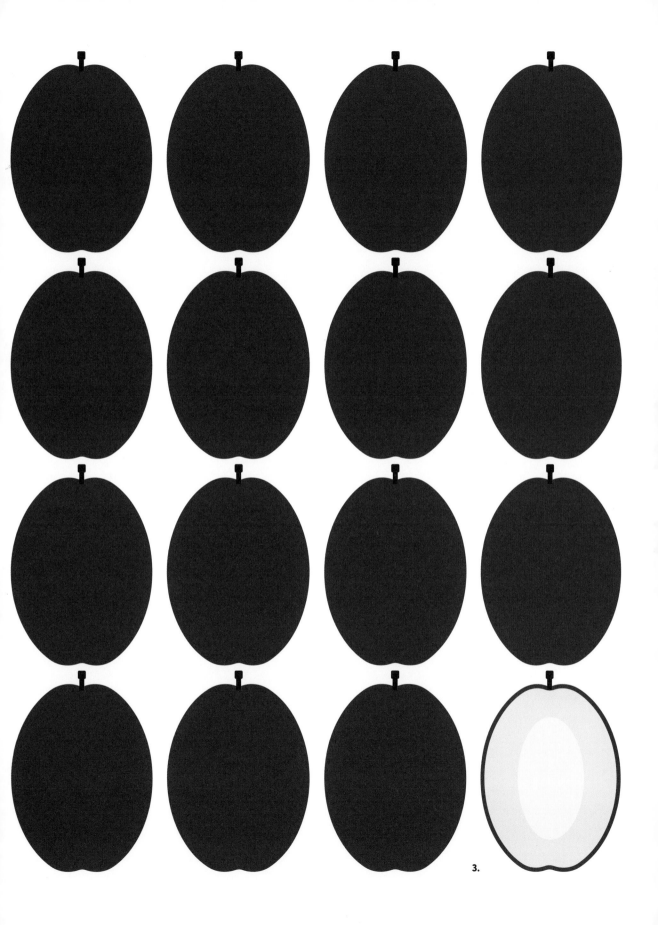

3.

Plum sauce

Makes about 4½ cups

This is my mum's recipe – a favourite with all the family and a great addition to a marinade or stir-fry.

....

Cut the plums in half and remove the stones. Place all the ingredients in a heavy-based saucepan and simmer, stirring occasionally, for 2–2½ hours until reduced and thickened.

Pass the mixture through the fine disc of a food mill, then pour into four or five warm sterilised 250 ml (8½ fl oz) bottles (see page 15). Wipe the rims and seal when cold. Leave the sauce to mature for at least 4 weeks before use. Refrigerate after opening.

1.5 kg (3 lb 5 oz) blood plums, halved, stones removed

850 ml (28½ fl oz) brown malt vinegar

650 g (1 lb 7 oz) sugar

2 teaspoons freshly ground pepper

3 teaspoons fine salt

¾ teaspoon ground cloves

¼ teaspoon cayenne pepper

1 teaspoon ground ginger

1 small garlic clove, peeled and left whole

4–5 x 250 ml (8½ fl oz) sterilised bottles

Cherries

Prunus avium (sweet)
Prunus cerasus (sour)

Cherries are available for such a fleeting moment that preserving these glistening red spheres can feel like a race against time. Luckily there are a multitude of ways to preserve this sublime fruit. Sour cherries can be dried, pickled or turned into jam; and sweet varieties are terrific for jams and pie filling.

Plant bareroot in late winter; container-grown in late autumn, early spring

Harvest summer, early autumn

Prune after fruiting in the first few summers

Needs cross-pollination yes

Bears first fruit third year

Pot yes, miniature and dwarf varieties

Aspect open, sunny position

Frost tolerant no

Soil pH 6.5–6.7

Cherries

1. Bing (sweet)
2. Napoleon (sweet)
3. St Margaret (sweet)
4. Morello (sour)

Nurture

Improve soil by digging in well-rotted manure and compost to a depth of 90 cm (3 feet) for sweet varieties, and a depth of 50 cm (1½ feet) for sour varieties. Stake when planting, feed with a complete fertiliser and mulch in spring. Cherries should be harvested by cutting – rather than pulling – the stalk from the tree to avoid damaging fruit spurs. Prune after fruiting for the first 3–4 years to remove long whippy shorts and to create a good framework. Long shoots with fruit clusters at the tip should be removed. Fruiting buds grow in clusters, while leaf buds appear separately along branches. Sweet cherry fruit will grow on one- and two-year-old wood. Sour cherries will develop on the previous year's wood.

Flavour companions

allspice, apricot, cinnamon, clove, coconut, ginger, lemon, nectarine, orange, peach, plum, quince, raspberry, vanilla

Pectin

sour, moderate; sweet, low

Ways to preserve

bottled, dried, pickled, jam, syrup, frozen

How to use

Dried sour cherries are fantastic added to muffins. Bottles of sweet varieties can be used in pies, warmed and poured over ice cream, or topped with fresh cream as a quick and delicious dessert. Don't dismiss the appeal of a simple frozen cherry, eaten with cream that has set as it is poured over the top. Arrange cherries in a single layer on a tray to freeze and then store them in a sealed container for snacking.

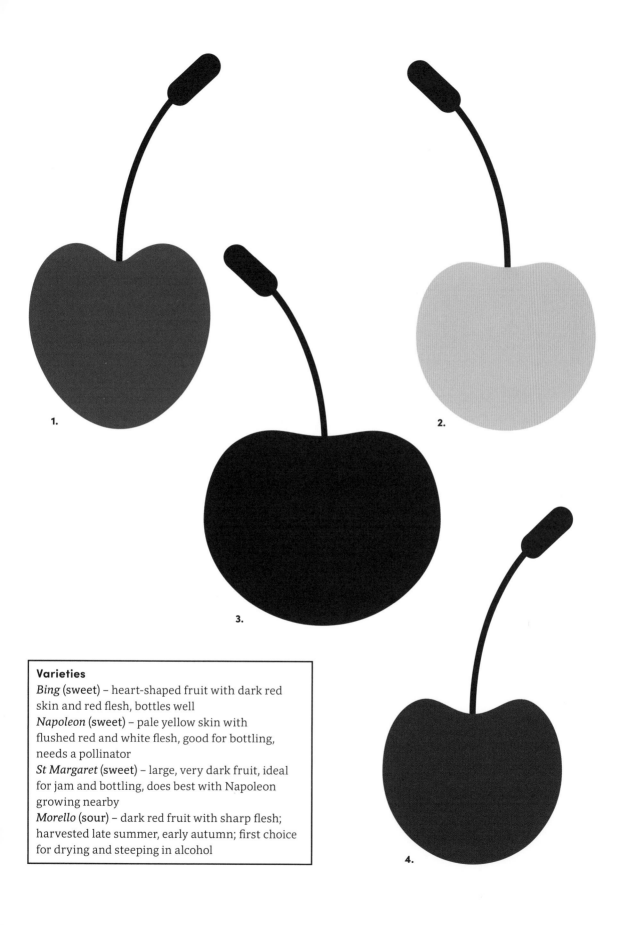

1.

2.

3.

4.

Varieties

Bing (sweet) – heart-shaped fruit with dark red skin and red flesh, bottles well

Napoleon (sweet) – pale yellow skin with flushed red and white flesh, good for bottling, needs a pollinator

St Margaret (sweet) – large, very dark fruit, ideal for jam and bottling, does best with Napoleon growing nearby

Morello (sour) – dark red fruit with sharp flesh; harvested late summer, early autumn; first choice for drying and steeping in alcohol

Dried sour cherries

If you don't have a dehydrator, it is possible to use the oven – or the sun – to dry cherries. Before you start, wash and dry the cherries, then remove the stems and stones.

Oven method
Preheat the oven to 80°C (175°F). Halve the cherries and place, cut side up, on large baking trays, leaving at least 2 cm (¾ inch) between each piece to allow air to circulate. Place in the oven for about 10 hours, then remove and cool completely on the trays. Store the dried cherries in sterilised jars (see page 15). If you see any condensation, return the cherries to the oven for further drying.

If 10 hours in the oven gives you the horrors (as it does me), the sun-drying method may be more appealing. You will need a large frame covered with a fine net or wire. I use an old window screen that I have scrubbed clean.

Sun method
Check the weather forecast and look for a run of hot, dry days (you want clear skies and temperatures over 30°C/86°F). Prepare the cherries as described above, spread them on the screen and place them outside in full sun. I bring the fruit inside overnight and turn it over each morning before returning it to a sunny position. Continue until the fruit is dry. The time needed depends on the weather, but 3–4 days of bright sun and temperatures above 30°C (86°F) is a good guide. If there is a change in the weather, or you simply grow impatient, you can finish the drying process in the oven for a couple of hours, as above. Store the cherries in sterilised jars (see page 15), watching for condensation.

Whichever method you use, store the dried cherries in a cool, dark place.

Bottled cherries

There is no need to pit cherries for this recipe; I think whole fruit looks more appealing in the bottle (just remember they have stones when serving). If you do pit the fruit, do it over a bowl to collect the juices and add them to the bottle with the liquid.

Remove the stems and wash the cherries in a bowl of cold water, discarding any cracked or blemished fruit. Drain well and pit if you wish. Pack the fruit into warm sterilised jars (see page 15), gently tapping the jars on the countertop to help the fruit settle. Fill the jars with water, or a light syrup (see page 16) and any juices collected from pitting, leaving 1 cm (½ inch) headspace. Wipe the rims, seal the jars and process in a water bath for 25 minutes (see page 14). Refrigerate after opening.

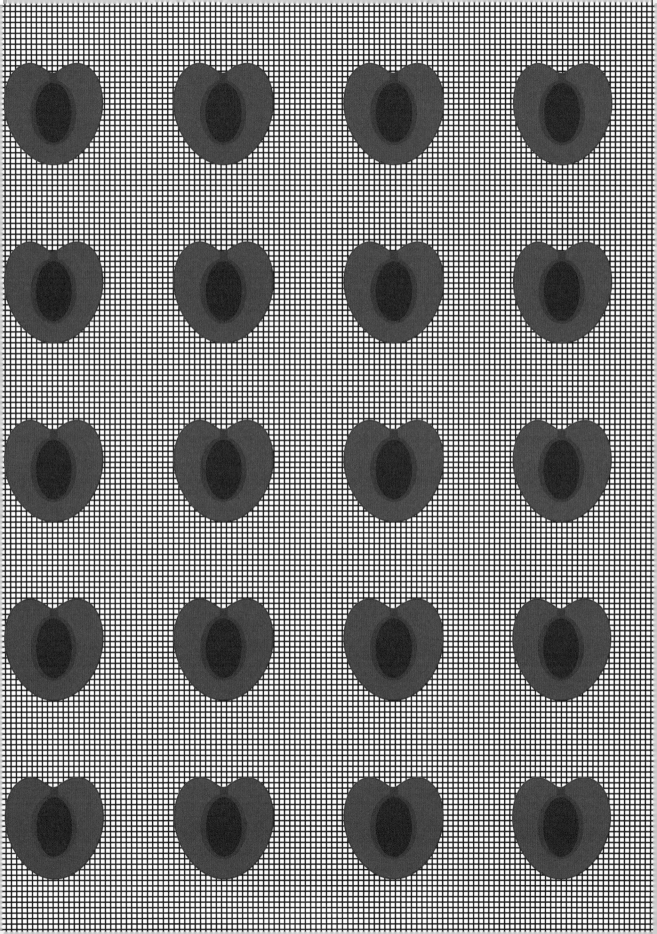

Figs

Ficus carica

It is not unusual to see huge, twisted fig trees on abandoned farms. Often, these enduring beauties will still produce fruit – proof of their tenacity and need for little ongoing care. Some fig varieties will even produce two crops a year.

Plant container-grown in late spring

Harvest summer, autumn

Prune twice a year, early to mid-spring

Needs cross-pollination no

Bears first fruit second year

Pot yes

Aspect warm, sunny position

Frost tolerant partially tolerant

Soil pH 7.0

Varieties
Black Genoa – squat, pear-shaped fruit with dark purple skin, red seeds and white flesh, good for jam
Brown Turkey – small to medium-sized fruit with distinctive ribs; purple-brown skin and sweet, pink-brown flesh, good preserved in syrup
White Adriatic – yellowish-green fruit and bright red flesh, excellent for jam, drying and bottling

Nurture
Create a rich, deep soil with the addition of well-rotted manure and compost to ensure good drainage. Apply a high-potash fertiliser to the top of the soil in early spring; figs have shallow roots, so don't dig in. Feed with a high-potash liquid fertiliser during summer. Water regularly in spring and summer. Pinch out tips in early to mid-spring to encourage development of next year's fruit.

Flavour companions
apple, blackberry, cardamom, cinnamon, fennel seed, ginger, grape, honey, lemon, orange, peach, pear, raspberry, rosemary

Pectin
moderate

Ways to preserve
bottled, candied, jam, dried, syrup, frozen, chutney

How to use
cakes, pies, tarts, salads, cheese boards, pizza, in stuffing

Figs

1. Black Genoa
2. Brown Turkey
3. White Adriatic

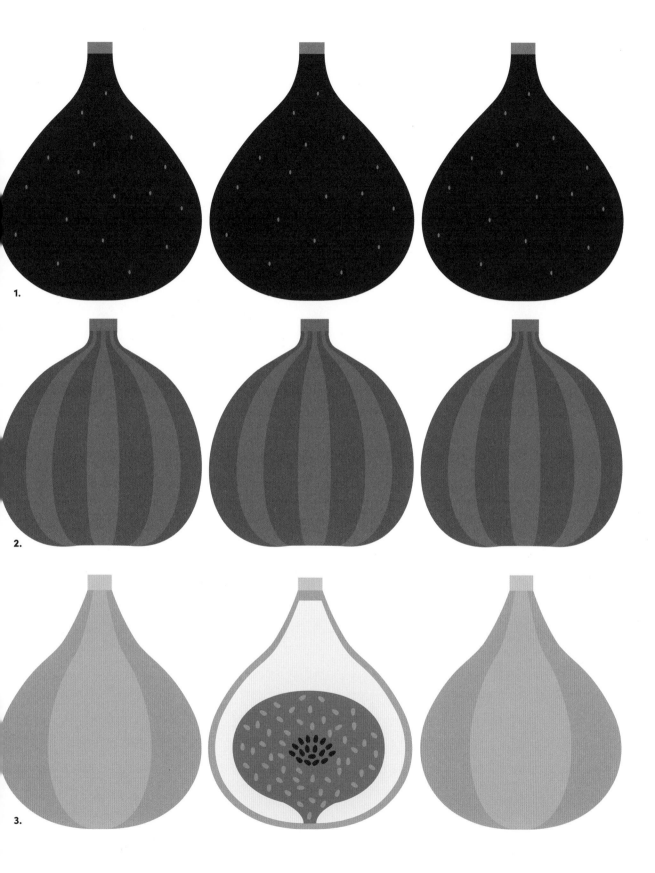

1.

2.

3.

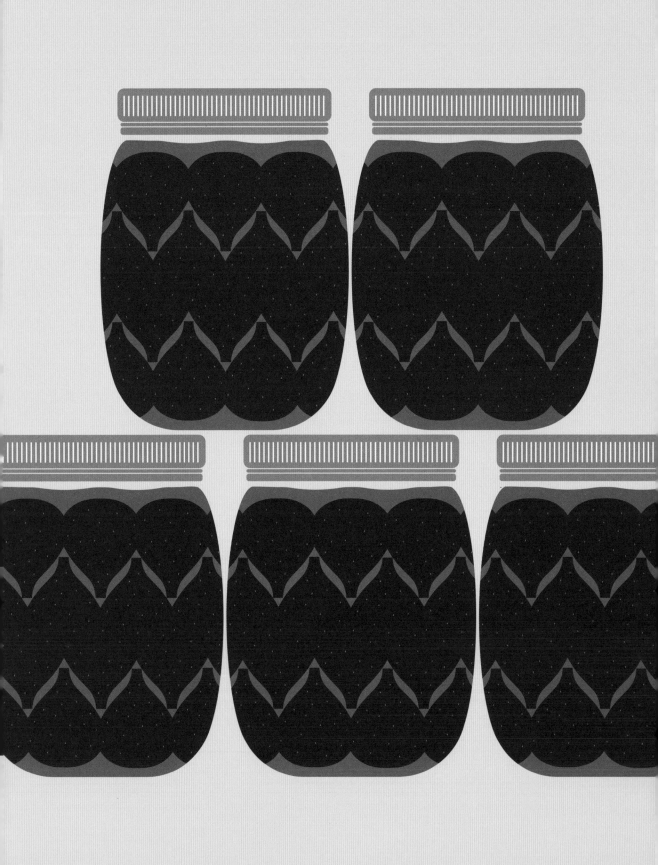

Figs in syrup

Heavy with syrup, these sweet figs are lovely served with soft, tangy cheeses and Greek yoghurt. Use small just-ripe figs that are still firm. Slices of lemon, orange or fresh ginger can all be added to the syrup.

1 kg (2 lb 3 oz) figs, washed and dried
800 g (1 lb 12 oz) sugar

3–4 x 300 ml (10 fl oz) sterilised jars

Remove the stems from the figs, then pierce the skin a few times with a toothpick.

Combine the sugar and 500 ml (1 pint) water in a heavy-based saucepan and bring to a slow boil over medium heat until the sugar has dissolved. Add the figs and simmer gently for 20 minutes.

Turn off the heat and allow the figs to cool completely in the syrup, then bring them back to a low simmer and cook for another 20 minutes. Gently place the figs in three or four warm sterilised 300 ml (10 fl oz) jars (see page 15) and cover with the syrup. Wipe the rims and seal when cold. Refrigerate after opening.

Olives

Olea europaea

Olives are incredibly hardy, drought-resistant trees. Slow-growing evergreens, they are beautiful when established, especially very old trees with twisted, gnarled trunks. In the home garden, they can be trained to grow against walls or fences, or clipped into hedges. Wind, rather than insects, pollinates olives, and while they are described as self-pollinating, fruit production is greatly improved by a second tree.

Plant winter

Harvest autumn

Prune annual, in early spring

Needs cross-pollination not essential

Bears first fruit third to fifth year

Pot yes, in a big pot

Aspect full sun

Frost tolerant yes

Soil pH 7.4–8.0

Varieties
Coratina – versatile and highly-productive variety, will thrive in a wide range of conditions, can be pickled when green or black, needs a pollinator
Manzanillo – excellent olive for pickling, great taste and texture, can be pickled when green or black, needs a pollinator
Picual – highly productive and very hardy medium-sized fruit, can be picked when green or black, needs a pollinator

Nurture
Plant olives into a moderately alkaline soil with good drainage. Stake plants well when planting. Apply a nitrogen-rich general-purpose fertiliser three times a year, water regularly when trees are establishing and monitor moisture during winter and spring when in flower and fruit is setting. Mulch with compost. Pot-grown olive trees should be fed with liquid fertiliser every 3–4 weeks during winter and spring. Prune to create and maintain shape and remove older branches to promote new growth. Fruit will grow on one-year-old wood.

Olive trees have become an environmental weed in some areas, so please consider the situation in your location before planting.

Flavour companions
chilli, coriander, cumin, fennel, garlic, lemon, onion, orange, oregano, parsley, pepper, thyme, tomato

Ways to preserve
pickled, dried, paste

How to use
Dried olives are delicious chopped up and sprinkled on salads, pastas and pizzas. Olive paste (tapenade) is great on some nice crusty bread or meat, and is a tasty addition to a cheese board.

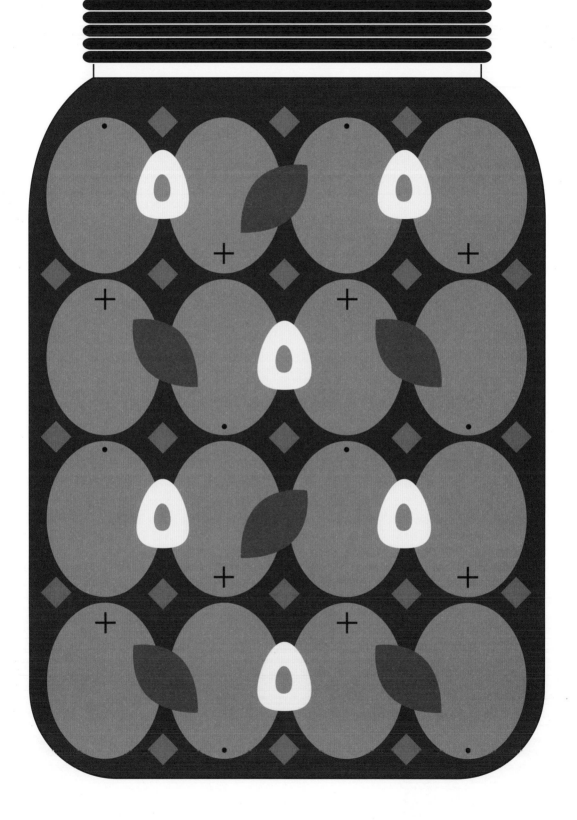

Spicy olives

This is a recipe of three parts: soaking, brining and marinating. While the process is not demanding and requires little hands-on time, it will take almost 2 months until the olives are ready to eat. The choice, quantity and combination of flavourings in the marinade is up to you – once the olives have been brined, divide them into smaller quantities and experiment with different marinades.

1 kg (2 lb 3 oz) olives, washed and pitted
60 g (¼ cup) fine salt
1 litre (1 quart) red wine vinegar
olive oil, to cover

Flavourings
garlic cloves, sliced
chilli flakes
strips of lemon rind
oregano sprigs

6–7 x 250 ml (8½ fl oz) sterilised jars

Place the olives in a large jar and cover with cold water. Drain and cover with fresh water every day for 2 weeks or until the olives are no longer too bitter to eat.

When they are pleasingly bitter, drain and place the olives in a large sterilised jar (see page 15). To make a brine, combine the salt and 1 litre (1 quart) water in a large saucepan and warm over low heat until the salt has dissolved. Set aside to cool. Add the vinegar to the brine and pour into the jar to cover the olives. Cover the surface of the brine with a thin layer of olive oil. Wipe the rim, seal the jar and leave in a cool, dark place for 1 month.

Wash and drain the brined olives, then layer them in six or seven warm sterilised 250 ml (8½ fl oz) jars (see page 15) with sliced garlic, chilli flakes, a strip of lemon rind and a small sprig of oregano (or any combination of these). Cover with olive oil, wipe the rims and seal. Refrigerate for at least 2 days and up to 1 week before using. Store in the fridge for 3 months.

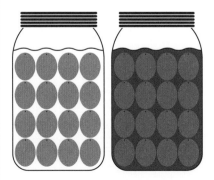

Walnuts

Juglans regia

The flavour and quality of any homegrown nut are always better than those offered for sale in greengrocers or supermarkets, and the walnut is perhaps the very best proof of this. You really do need a big garden to grow these. The large evergreen tree is a handsome feature when allowed to spread and grow to its full potential of 18–20 metres (59–65 feet).

Plant late autumn, winter

Harvest autumn

Prune after the first or second year

Needs cross-pollination not essential

Bears first fruit fourth to fifth year

Pot no

Aspect full sun

Frost tolerant yes, although flowers are damaged by spring frost

Soil pH 6.5–7.0

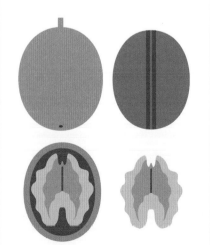

Varieties
Chandler – light-coloured kernels held in large, tightly sealed nuts
Persian/English – beautifully flavoured, large nuts
Howard – large, smooth nuts, most with light-coloured flesh, small to medium in size, good choice for backyards

Nurture
Walnuts secrete a chemical that can inhibit the growth of other plants and should be situated to avoid this happening. Plant into deep, well-drained and moist soil. Stake when planting and apply a balanced fertiliser in early spring. Mulch after planting and then annually. Prune young trees only when necessary to establish their shape and remove dead branches. Prune established trees annually to removed broken or crowded branches. The trees produce both male and female flowers and are pollinated by the wind. However, flower and nut production will improve with a second walnut tree nearby. Recipes for pickled walnuts use 'green' walnuts; this refers to the nut before the outer casing has hardened. If you are not going to use them within a week of harvesting, store shelled nuts in the freezer for up to 12 months.

Flavour companions
apple, chocolate, cinnamon, fig, nutmeg, orange, peach, pear, plum, vanilla

Ways to preserve
candied, pickled (green), frozen

How to use
cheese boards, syrup, added to beef stew, in desserts

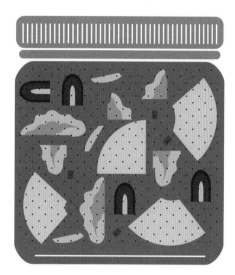

Apple and walnut chutney

Makes about 4½ cups

A natural on a cheese board, this chutney improves with age. It can also be added to a rich beef stew or stirred through yoghurt to eat with curry.

Peel, core and roughly chop the apples. Place in a heavy-based saucepan with the onion, chilli, sugar and vinegar and stir over low heat until the sugar has dissolved. Add the ginger, cinnamon and salt and bring to a gentle boil. Cook, stirring occasionally, until the apple has softened and a spatula or wooden spoon dragged through the centre of the mixture leaves a clear path without any liquid pooling on the base of the pan. Stir regularly so the mixture doesn't catch and burn.

While the apple is cooking, place the walnuts in a dry frying pan over low heat and roast until aromatic, stirring constantly as they can burn easily.

When the chutney is ready, add the walnuts and cook, stirring, for a few minutes. Spoon into four or five warm sterilised 250 ml (8½ fl oz) jars (see page 15). Wipe the rims and seal when cold. Refrigerate after opening.

1 kg (2 lb 3 oz) apples
2 onions, finely sliced
1 bird's eye chilli (or to taste), seeds removed, chopped
250 g (9 oz) brown sugar
125 ml (½ cup) brown malt vinegar
80 g (2¾ oz) pitted dates, roughly chopped
3 teaspoons ground ginger
½ teaspoon ground cinnamon
½ teaspoon fine salt
80 g (2¾ oz) shelled walnuts, roughly chopped

4–5 x 250 ml (8½ fl oz) sterilised jars

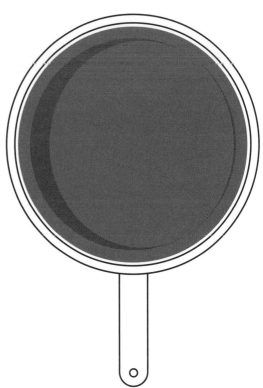
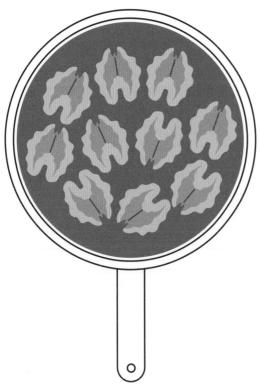
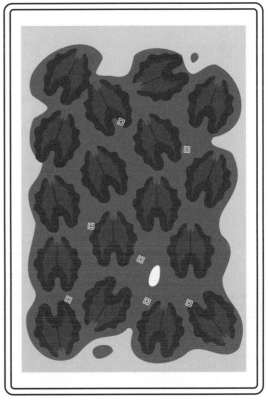

Candied walnuts

When I was growing up candied walnuts were always a Christmas treat. I'm unsure if they were unavailable at other times of the year, but this was the only time I remember having them. They are incredibly moreish eaten as they are, but are also lovely as part of a cheese board, chopped and sprinkled over a salad, or used to decorate the top of a cake.

300 g (3 cups) shelled walnuts
220 g (1 cup) brown sugar
¼ teaspoon fine salt

3–4 x 250 ml (8½ fl oz) sterilised jars

....

Preheat the oven to 175°C (345°F). Line two baking trays with baking paper.

Spread the walnuts over one of the lined trays in a single layer, then roast for 5 minutes or until aromatic and slightly darkened. Keep an eye on them; they can go from perfect to ruined in seconds. Remove and set aside to cool.

Place the sugar in a heavy-based saucepan over medium–low heat and cook, gently swirling the pan, until it has dissolved and darkened to an amber colour. Add the walnuts and, working quickly, stir to coat them in the toffee. Tip the walnuts onto the second tray and sprinkle with salt, then use two forks to pull the nuts apart and arrange them in a single layer. Leave to cool and set, then store in three or four sterilised 250 ml (8½ fl oz) jars (see page 15). Candied walnuts will keep in the fridge for up to 1 month.

Almonds

Prunus dulcis

The spring blossoms and edible nuts of the almond tree are a double delight for gardeners. This deciduous tree is self–fertile and available in a dwarf or multi–grafted forms, with dwarf varieties suited to small gardens or growing in pots.

Plant bareroot in late autumn, winter; potted, year round

Harvest autumn

Prune annual, spring or summer

Needs cross-pollination no

Bears first fruit third to fourth year

Pot yes, dwarf and miniature varieties

Aspect full sun

Frost tolerant partially, early spring frost will damage flowers

Soil pH 6.5–7.0

Varieties
Zaione – heavy cropping, self-pollinating, sweet, soft-shelled
Chellaston – soft-shelled, dark skin, sweet and oval-shaped, self-fertile, needs cross pollinator
Ne Plus Ultra – large, papershell, light chocolate colour, heavy cropping, excellent pollinator for other almond varieties

Nurture
Choose a sunny position that is protected from strong winds with good drainage and plant in late autumn into deep soil enriched with well-rotted manure or compost. Stake when planting, applying a layer of mulch around the base of the tree avoiding the trunk. Feed annually in late winter with a general-purpose fertiliser. Keep moist during growing season. Feed almonds growing in pots with liquid or slow-release fertiliser during the growing season. Replace the top layer of soil with fresh potting mix or repot into a larger container every year. Nuts are produced on previous year's wood. Prune annually in spring or summer to generate new growth and maintain an open centre.

Flavour companions
apple, apricot, blackberry, blackcurrant, blueberry, cardamom, cherry, cinnamon, fig, garlic, ginger, grape, nectarine, olive, peach, pear, raspberry, rhubarb, strawberry

Ways to preserve
butter, candied, frozen, pickled (green)

How to use
baking

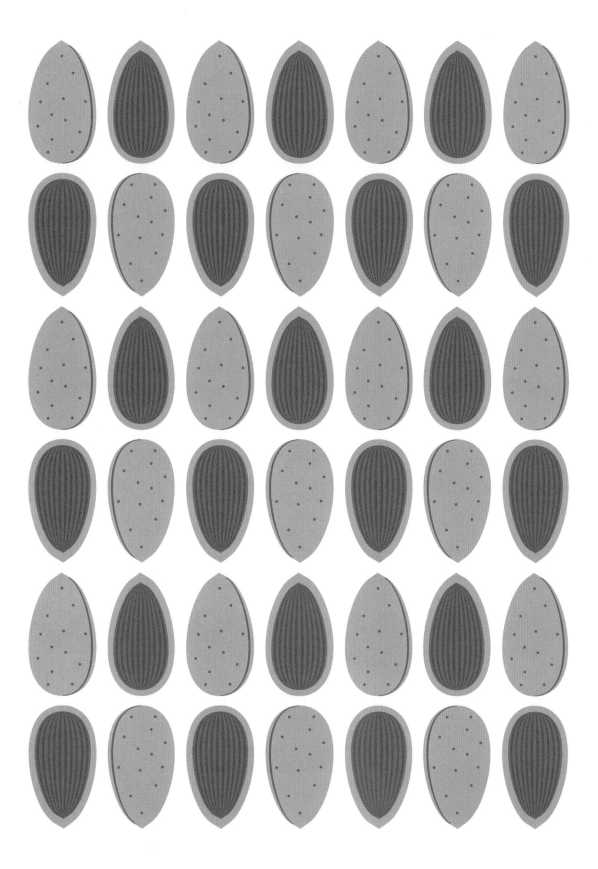

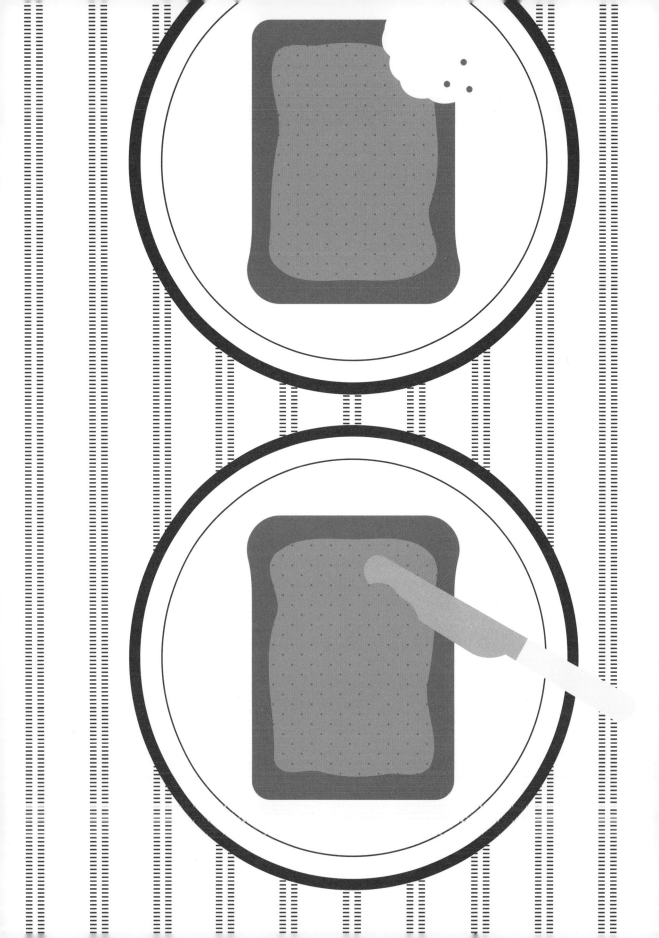

Almond butter

Makes about 1½ cups

Making your own nut butter allows you to calibrate the level of crunchiness, add salt and sugar to taste and experiment with other flavours. Try adding maple syrup, honey, cinnamon or vanilla to create a 'house butter'. Roasting the almonds first heightens their flavour and makes them easier to blend.

500 g (1 lb 2 oz) natural almonds
¼ teaspoon fine salt

2 x 200 ml (7 fl oz) sterilised jars

Preheat the oven to 175°C (345°F). Line a baking tray with baking paper.

Spread the almonds over the lined tray in a single layer and roast for 10 minutes or until aromatic, turning them over halfway through. Remove and set aside to cool slightly. If you prefer a crunchy texture, keep 2–3 tablespoons of the roasted almonds aside. Add them once a paste has formed, then blitz until your desired consistency is achieved.

While the nuts are still warm, place them in a food processor or blender and blitz until the butter is as smooth or as crunchy as you like, occasionally stopping and scraping down the side. Be patient: the nuts will become a dry meal, then form a ball and finally transform into a paste. When the paste is your desired consistency, add the salt (and any other flavourings) and mix in with a rubber spatula.

Allow the almond butter to cool, then spoon into two warm sterilised 200 ml (7 fl oz) jars (see page 15). Store in the fridge for up to 2 weeks, or freeze for longer storage.

Passionfruit

Passiflora edulis

Passionfruit are everywhere and in a seemingly endless supply – until they are not. Growing your own passionfruit vine will lesson this seasonal scarcity. You can freeze the whole fruit or remove the pulp and freeze it in an ice cube tray. I prefer to preserve small jars of the unsweetened pulp ready to pour over fruit salad, mix into the icing for a celebratory sponge cake, or, of course, as a final flourish on a classic pavlova.

Plant spring

Harvest summer, autumn

Prune light annual, vines can be trimmed in early spring to encourage new growth

Needs cross-pollination yes, some varieties

Bears first fruit second to third year

Pot yes, large pot with supportive structure

Aspect full sun

Frost tolerant yes, once established

Soil pH 6.5–7.5

Passionfruit

1. Sweet Granadilla
2. Nellie Kelly
3. Misty Gem

Varieties
Sweet Granadilla – yellow skin and delicious, sweet pulp
Nellie Kelly – reliable, grafted variety that produces fruit for months
Misty Gem – bright yellow to deep golden pulp with fabulous flavour

Nurture
Passionfruit need a sturdy support and should be sheltered from strong and cold winds. Vines are fast-growing and are a great way to screen an unsightly wall or fence. Young plants should be protected from frost. Soil must have excellent drainage and should be enriched with lots of well-rotted chicken or cow manure and compost before planting. Feed with well-rotted chicken manure or a high-potash fertiliser in autumn and spring to encourage fruit production, mulch to reduce moisture loss. If you keep chickens, plant a passionfruit vine on the coop fence – the ready supply of manure and straw will see the vine thrive.

Flavour companions
coriander, ginger, lemon, lime, mango, orange, peach, pear, pineapple, strawberry, vanilla

Pectin
low

Ways to preserve
frozen (whole, or separate pulp and place in ice cube trays), jam, bottled, dehydrated

How to use
baking, desserts

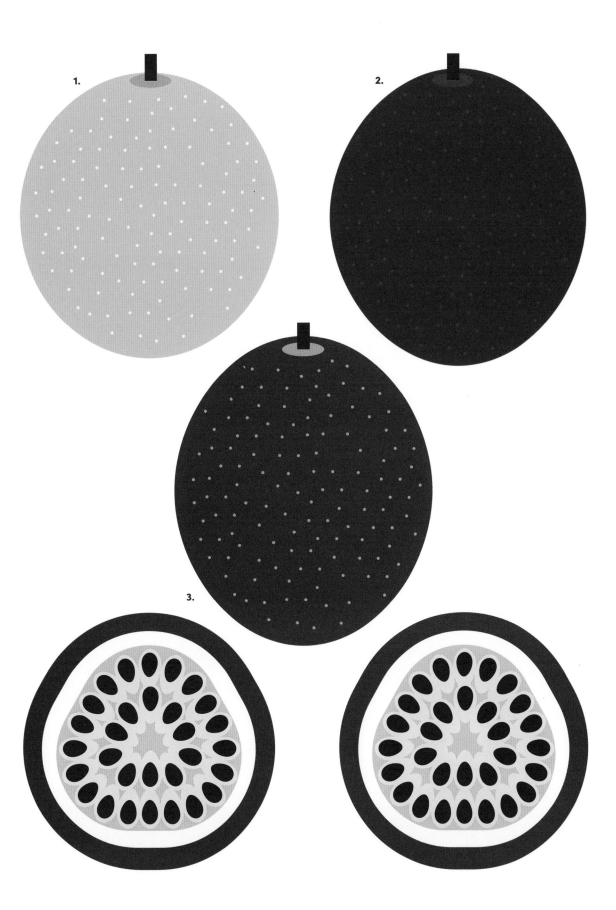

1.

2.

3.

Preserved passionfruit pulp

Makes about 2½ cups

When I can I like to use small round-bottomed jars when preserving this pulp, for no other reason than the plump bases mimic the shape of the whole fruit and make me smile. A ready supply of unsweetened passionfruit opens a world of baking possibilities throughout the year.

1 kg (2 lb 3 oz) passionfruit, washed, stalks removed

5–6 125 ml (4 fl oz) sterilised jars

Rather than cutting the passionfruit in half, slice the tops off (as you would a boiled egg) and scoop the pulp into a jug or bowl.

Fill five or six warm sterilised 125 ml (4 fl oz) jars (see page 15) with the pulp, leaving 1 cm (½ inch) headspace, wipe the rims and seal the jars before processing in a water bath. Note: the process here is a little different. The water should be warm when you add the jars, then brought to the boil and processed for 15 minutes. Refrigerate after opening and use within 1 week.

Raspberries

Rubus idaeus

I think raspberries were the first crop I grew that produced enough fruit to send me looking for ways to use it. Some varieties will fruit twice a year, and while there are yellow and white varieties, nothing beats the red fruit's colour, perfume and flavour. A ready supply of homegrown raspberries is a joy. Relatively easy to grow, these wild and prolific berries always feature in summer recipes, but growing and preserving your own ensures the sweet, tart fruit is available throughout the year.

Plant early spring

Harvest summer

Prune annual, after fruiting

Needs cross-pollination no

Bears first fruit first year

Pot yes, in large container or trough

Aspect full sun to part shade

Frost tolerant yes

Soil pH 5.5–6.5

Nurture

Boost soil before planting with the addition of generous amounts of well-rotted manure and compost. Plant canes running north to south at a spacing of 75 cm (2½ feet) with vertical support around 1 m (3 feet) high. Erect two poles and thread them with rows of wire or strong garden twine every 20 cm (8 inches). Raspberries do best in well-drained, rich, loamy soil and a situation that is protected from hot winds. Water well and mulch with straw after planting, keep soil moist. Apply a light layer of all-purpose fertiliser in spring and water deeply while fruit is growing. Raspberries have surface roots so the soil should not be dug, instead mulch with a thick layer of manure or compost and a layer of straw after pruning. Autumn-fruiting varieties that bear on the current year's wood should be cut at ground level. Summer-fruiting varieties bear on second year's wood; cut canes that have produced fruit to the ground, leaving five to six new canes per plant.

Flavour companions

citrus, ginger, mint, redcurrant, rhubarb, strawberry, thyme, vanilla

Pectin

moderate

Ways to preserve

jam, jelly, frozen, dehydrated, vinegar

How to use

salad dressing, vinaigrette, on pancakes, diluted in soda water, baking, desserts

Varieties
Chilliwack – an excellent backyard variety with almost thornless canes and sizeable red fruit in summer
Willamette – high-yielding with two crops of rich red fruit in summer and autumn
Autumn Bliss – large, sweet fruit born on new growth, easy to maintain

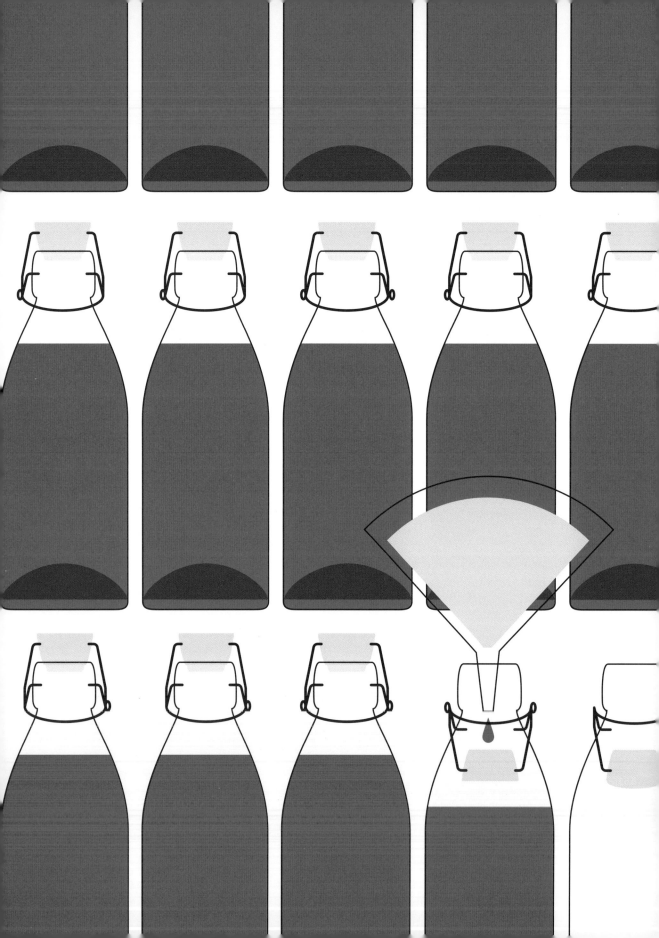

Raspberry vinegar

Makes about 2½ cups

It was a now-forgotten book that alerted me to the existence of raspberry vinegar – a simple cordial exploding with the intense flavour of my favourite summer fruit. As the fruit steeps, the house fills with the unmistakable fragrance of this deep red berry. I prefer it on the tart side, but by all means increase the sugar to suit your taste. Raspberry vinegar can be used in salad dressings or simply diluted with soda water for a stunning thirst quencher. It's also incredibly good drizzled over fresh strawberries.

500 g (1 lb 2 oz) raspberries
500 ml (1 pint) apple cider vinegar
300 g (10½ oz) sugar (or to taste)

2–3 x 250 ml (8½ fl oz) sterilised bottles

Place the raspberries and vinegar in a non-reactive bowl and gently squash them with a potato masher. Cover and steep in a cool, dark place for 4–7 days, by which time the incredible perfume of raspberries will be unmistakable.

To strain, pour the mixture into a square of clean muslin sitting in a colander, then gather up the sides and secure with string. Suspend the muslin over a bowl, leaving it to drip overnight. Resist the temptation to squeeze the fruit as this will produce a cloudy vinegar.

Combine the extracted juice and sugar in a heavy-based saucepan and stir over low heat until the sugar has dissolved, then increase the heat and bring to the boil. Pour the hot vinegar into two or three warm sterilised 250 ml (8½ fl oz) bottles (see page 15). I place a coffee filter in a funnel to remove stray pulp or pips. Seal the bottles immediately and store in a cool, dark place. Dilute before drinking and refrigerate after opening.

Blackberries

Rubus fruticosus

In some places, blackberries are an invasive environmental weed. When I was young, huge brambles lined roads and paddocks, offering an annual bounty of fruit. Widespread removal efforts mean this is no longer possible. If you do see roadside fruit, resist the urge to pick it; chances are it may be sprayed with poison. Thankfully, sterile cultivars are now available to grow in the home garden.

♈	**Plant** winter, early spring
◎	**Harvest** late summer, early autumn
✂	**Prune** annual, after fruiting
✿✿	**Needs cross-pollination** no
♂	**Bears first fruit** first year
▽	**Pot** no
☀	**Aspect** full sun to part shade
✳	**Frost tolerant** yes
⚱	**Soil pH** 6.8–7.5

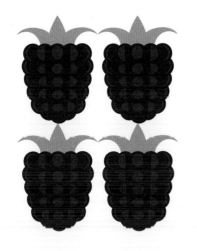

Varieties
Chester – vigorous canes produce sweet, flavourful fruit throughout summer, minimal thorns

Nurture
Plant into rich, well-drained soil that has been dug through with manure and compost and in a situation that is protected from strong winds. Blackberry canes should be planted with a strong support. Erect two poles and thread them with rows of wire or strong garden twine every 90 cm (3 feet). Plant canes 1 m (3½ feet) apart, water well and mulch with a layer of straw after planting. In spring, feed with an all-purpose fertiliser or apply a layer of manure or compost and mulch with straw. Keep plants moist.

Fruit is produced on second-year wood, meaning plants can be pruned any time after fruiting. Cut old canes to the ground leaving five to six strong new canes per plant. Tie canes to support after pruning.

Flavour companions
apple, apricot, blueberry, cinnamon, clove, ginger, lemon, mint, mulberry, orange, peach, pear, raspberry, strawberry, vanilla

Pectin
moderate

Ways to preserve
bottled, dehydrated (whole, chopped or powdered), jam, frozen

How to use
baking, desserts, pie filling

Blackberry and apple filling

Makes about 3½ cups

This fruity concoction is perfect for an impromptu crumble. Discovering a jar in the pantry can feel like a big win when time is short and culinary inspiration has vanished.

500 g (1 lb 2 oz) apples
2 tablespoons sugar
400 g (14 oz) blackberries

1 x 1 litre (1 quart) sterilised jar

Peel, core and slice the apples into large wedges. Place in a heavy-based saucepan with the sugar and 60 ml (¼ cup) water and cook, covered, over medium heat until the apple has softened, stirring occasionally. Mix in the blackberries.

Spoon the hot mixture into a 1 litre (1 quart) warm sterilised jar (see page 15), leaving 1 cm (½ inch) headspace. Remove any air bubbles by gently running a small spatula down and around the side of the jar. Wipe the rim, seal the jar and process in a water bath for 30 minutes (see page 14). Store in a cool, dark place. The filling will keep for up to 12 months if properly preserved.

When you are you ready to whip up a dessert, blend 2 teaspoons cornflour (cornstarch) and 1 tablespoon water and stir through the filling. Top with your favourite crumble, cobbler dough or pastry and bake.

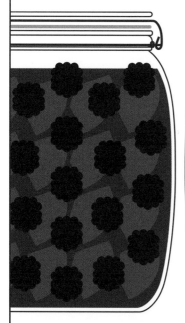

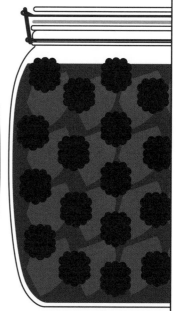

Blueberries

Vaccinium cyanococcus

I struggled for years to grow blueberries; it wasn't until I decided to plant them in large containers – where I could control the soil pH and create an acid growing medium – that I had any success.

🌱 **Plant** autumn, spring

◎ **Harvest** late summer, autumn

✂ **Prune** annual, after leaves have fallen

❀❀ **Needs cross-pollination** fruit production is improved with cross-pollinator

♂ **Bears first fruit** first to second year

🪴 **Pot** yes, preferred

☀ **Aspect** full sun

❄ **Frost tolerant** yes

⚘ **Soil pH** 4.0–5.5

Varieties
Sunshine Blue – compact, productive shrub, bears medium-sized fruit in summer
O'Neal – large sweet fruit with good flavour, heat tolerant plants with grey–green foliage
Brightwell –vigorous, low-maintenance, drought- and heat-tolerant variety, early-fruiting

Nurture
Prepare soil well in advance of planting, blueberries prefer a free-draining soil with lots of well-rotted manure and compost added. If you are planting in the ground create a raised bed to improve drainage. Space plants 1.5 m (5 feet) apart. Water well and mulch after planting. Blueberries need regular, deep watering and should be fed with a balanced fertiliser and extra nitrogen after pruning. Reapply an acidic mulch every spring. Potted plants should be re-potted every second autumn. Watering with cold coffee and mulching with pine needles can help make alkaline soil more acid. When pruning, remove about a quarter of the growth, cutting to 2.5 cm (1 inch) above the soil. Remove any weak or damaged branches. When new buds are visible, cut one or two branches to ground level to encourage strong, new growth. Remove flowers for the first year to encourage strong growth.

Flavour companions
fig, ginger, honey, lemon, lime, nutmeg, orange, peach, vanilla

Pectin
low–moderate

Ways to preserve
jam, jelly, dehydrated (whole, chopped or powdered), frozen, sauces, syrup

How to use
baking, desserts

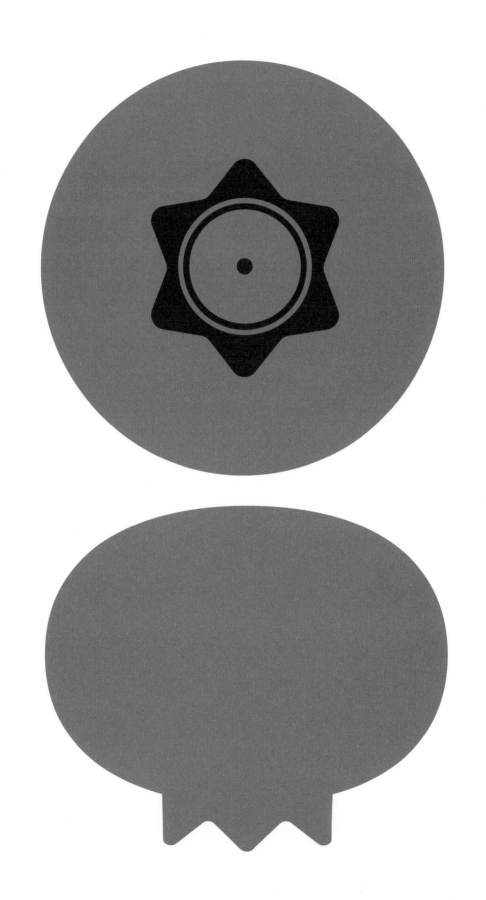

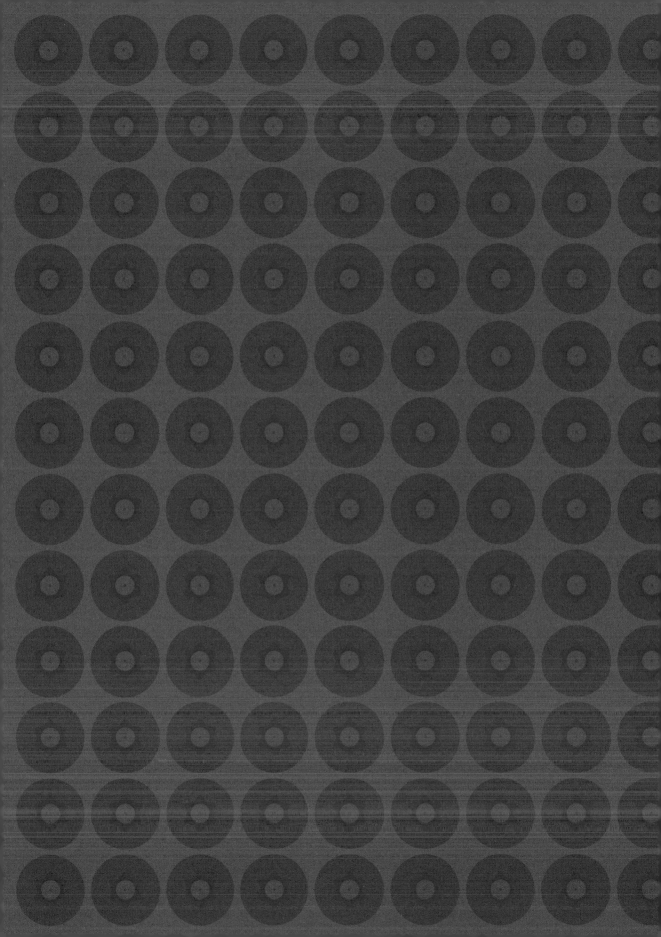

Blueberry jam

Makes about 3 cups

Always on the table when we have pancakes, this dark, fruit-packed jam is also delicious on scones or thickly spread with cream to sandwich a sponge cake.

500 g (1 lb 2 oz) blueberries
60 ml (¼ cup) freshly squeezed
   lemon juice
400 g (14 oz) sugar

3 x 250 ml (8½ fl oz) sterilised jars

Place a small saucer in the freezer. Combine the blueberries and lemon juice in a heavy-based saucepan and simmer, covered, over medium heat for 15 minutes or until the fruit has softened. Add the sugar and stir without boiling until the sugar has dissolved. Bring to the boil and cook for another 15 minutes or until a set is achieved.

To test, remove the pan from the heat and place a spoonful of jam on the cold saucer. Pop the saucer back in the freezer for a couple of minutes – if the jam wrinkles when pushed, it is ready. If not, cook for another 5 minutes and test again. Pour the jam into three warm sterilised 250 ml (8½ fl oz) jars (see page 15), wipe the rims and seal when cold. Refrigerate after opening.

Strawberries

Fragaria

Perfect for growing in pots, hanging baskets or in a vertical garden, strawberries are the gardener's treat: sweet jewels to pick and eat as you work. If you can't pick a large enough quantity at the one time, simply freeze strawberries on a tray lined with baking paper, storing the harvest until you have what you need to make jam.

♈	**Plant** summer, autumn, spring
◎	**Harvest** spring, summer, autumn
✄	**Prune** annual, after fruiting
⚥	**Needs cross-pollination** fruit production is improved with cross-pollinator
♂	**Bears first fruit** first year
⛾	**Pot** yes
☼	**Aspect** full sun, part shade
✳	**Frost tolerant** yes, plants are dormant in winter
⏚	**Soil pH** 5.5–6.5

Varieties

Reine des Vallees – alpine variety with fragrant red fruit and amazing flavour
Tioga – vigorous variety, produces large crops of bright red fruit through spring and summer
Rubygem – large, dark red fruit from autumn to early spring, grows well in a climate with mild winters

Nurture

Well before planting create a rich, free-draining soil with the addition of well-rotted manure, compost and all-purpose fertiliser. Plant crowns level to the soil surface, gently extending any runners and covering these with soil at 30 cm (1 foot) intervals. Water well until they produce new leaves, during dry periods and when fruit is swelling. Apply a high-potash liquid fertiliser a month after planting, then a balanced liquid fertiliser every 2 weeks until flowers appear. Once fruit forms, avoid watering overhead to protect it from spoiling. Mulch annually with compost. Strawberries growing in containers should be fertilised with slow-release fertiliser in spring.

Flavour companions

apple, apricot, balsamic vinegar, basil, blackberry, blueberry, boysenberry, cardamom, cinnamon, clove, coriander, cumquat, ginger, gooseberry, grape, grapefruit, lemon, lime, mint, nutmeg, orange, passionfruit, peach, pineapple, plum, pomegranate, raspberry, rhubarb, vanilla

Pectin

low

Ways to preserve

jam, jelly, dehydrated (whole, chopped or powdered), frozen, sauce, syrup

How to use

baking, desserts

Strawberry jam

I no longer try to make strawberry jam without the help of powdered pectin. Countless hours cooking, waiting and testing only ever resulted in a disappointing runny mixture. Even with the pectin this is not a firm jam. While the flavour of strawberries alone is delightful, you could also add a vanilla bean, lime zest or black pepper while the jam is cooking, or stir through balsamic vinegar or finely chopped tarragon or basil just before pouring the jam into jars.

Place a small saucer in the freezer. Combine the strawberries, lemon juice and pectin in a heavy-based saucepan and cook, stirring, over medium heat for 10 minutes or until the fruit has softened. Add the sugar and stir until it has dissolved, then increase the heat and boil rapidly, stirring occasionally, for 15–20 minutes.

To test for set, remove the pan from the heat and place a spoonful of jam on the cold saucer. Pop the saucer back in the freezer for a couple of minutes – if the jam wrinkles when pushed, it is ready. If not, cook for another 5 minutes, stirring as it comes back to the boil so the fruit doesn't stick to the bottom of the pan, and test again.

When the jam is at setting point, turn off the heat and allow it to sit for 10–15 minutes. Skim off any foam, then pour the jam into four warm sterilised 250 ml (8½ fl oz) jars (see page 15), leaving 1 cm (½ inch) headspace if processing in a water bath. Wipe the rims. If you choose not to process the jam in a water bath allow the jam to cool completely before sealing the jars. Otherwise, seal the jars immediately and process in a water bath for 15 minutes (see page 14). Refrigerate after opening.

750 g (1 lb 11 oz) strawberries, washed and hulled, or frozen strawberries (no need to thaw)
60 ml (¼ cup) freshly squeezed lemon juice
2 tablespoons powdered pectin
350 g (12½ oz) sugar

4 x 250 ml (8½ fl oz) sterilised jars

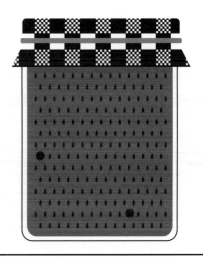

Strawberry and rhubarb jam

Makes about 5 cups

Strawberries and rhubarb are a match made in heaven – the combination of sweet and tart flavours produce a jam that is so much more than the sum of its parts.

Place a small saucer in the freezer. Combine the fruit, lemon juice and pectin in a heavy-based saucepan. Cover and cook over low heat, stirring occasionally, for 15 minutes or until the fruit has softened to a pulp. Add the sugar and stir until it has dissolved, then increase the heat and boil, stirring occasionally, for 10–15 minutes.

To test for set, remove the pan from the heat and place a spoonful of jam on the cold saucer. Pop the saucer back in the freezer for a couple of minutes – if the jam wrinkles when pushed, it is ready. If not, cook for another 5 minutes, stirring as it comes back to the boil so the fruit doesn't stick to the bottom of the pan, and test again.

When the jam is at setting point, turn off the heat and allow it to sit for 10 minutes. Skim off any foam, then pour the jam into five or six warm sterilised 250 ml (8½ fl oz) jars (see page 15), leaving 1 cm (½ inch) headspace if processing in a water bath. Wipe the rims. If you choose not to process the jam in a water bath allow the jam to cool completely before sealing the jars. Otherwise, seal the jars immediately and process in a water bath for 15 minutes (see page 14). Refrigerate after opening.

750 g (1 lb 11 oz) strawberries, washed and hulled, or frozen strawberries (no need to thaw)

500 g (1 lb 2 oz) rhubarb, washed and cut into 2.5 cm (1 inch) pieces

60 ml (¼ cup) freshly squeezed lemon juice

2 tablespoons powdered pectin

350 g (12½ oz) sugar

5–6 x 250 ml (8½ fl oz) sterilised jars

Gooseberries

Ribes uva-crispa

Gooseberries make a lovely tart jam that varies in colour from green to pink depending on the variety and ripeness of the fruit. High pectin and acid levels make a jam that sets quickly, making gooseberries a useful addition to jams and jellies made with low-pectin fruits.

☿	**Plant** autumn, early spring
◎	**Harvest** summer
✂	**Prune** annual
❦❦	**Needs cross-pollination** no
♂	**Bears first fruit** second to third year
⊔	**Pot** yes
☼	**Aspect** full sun
✳	**Frost tolerant** yes
⏚	**Soil pH** 6.5–7.3

Varieties
Captivator – almost thornless bush with sweet purple-red fruit when ripe
Whinham's Industry – sweet, all-purpose fruit with large, dark red berries

Nurture
Plant this deciduous perennial into soil that has been boosted with well-rotted manure and compost. Fertilise with a high-potash fertiliser in spring and summer. Mulch to help keep soil moist and water well during dry weather. In winter, cut plants back to three or four shoots in the first year, and six to eight shoots in the following years.

Flavour companions
apple, bay leaf, coriander, lemon, mint, mustard, orange, strawberry, vanilla

Pectin
high

Ways to preserve
chutney, jam, jelly, frozen (whole or pureed)

How to use
Chutney is great paired with cheese or oily fish. Jam is delicious spread on toast or muffins, and is fantastic spooned on top of ice cream.

Gooseberry jam

Makes about 4 cups

Gooseberries remain green when ripe and fruit picked early in the season will produce a green-hued jam, while late season fruit produces a glorious pinkish result. The high pectin content of gooseberries means jam making is easy and makes them a useful addition to fruit with poor setting qualities. Try swapping 500g (1 lb 2 oz) of strawberries for half the quantity of gooseberries in this recipe.

1 kg (2 lb 3 oz) gooseberries, washed

60 ml (¼ cup) freshly squeezed lemon juice

1 kg (2 lb 3 oz) sugar

4 x 250 ml (8½ fl oz) sterilised jars

Place a small saucer in the freezer. Combine the gooseberries, lemon juice and 125 ml (½ cup) water in a heavy-based saucepan. Cover and cook over medium heat, stirring occasionally, for 15 minutes or until the fruit has softened to a pulp. Reduce the heat to low, add the sugar and stir until it has dissolved, then increase the heat and boil, stirring occasionally, for about 10 minutes.

To test for set, remove the pan from the heat and place a spoonful of jam on the cold saucer. Pop the saucer back in the freezer for a couple of minutes – if the jam wrinkles when pushed, it is ready. If not, cook for another 5 minutes and test again.

When the jam is at setting point, turn off the heat and allow it to sit for 10 minutes. Skim off any foam, then pour the jam into four warm sterilised 250 ml (8½ fl oz) jars (see page 15). Wipe the rims and seal when cold. Store in a cool, dark place and refrigerate after opening.

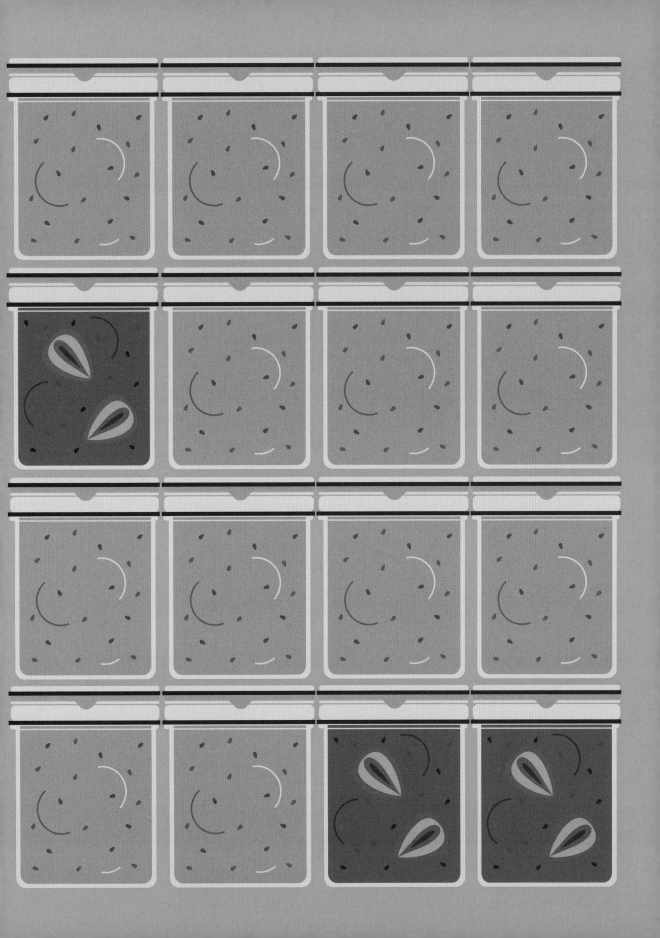

Mulberries

Where I live, there seems to be at least one mulberry tree in every backyard, often massive spreading specimens with canopies that create shady alcoves large enough to hide a table and chairs or create a magical cubby. The size and prevalence of these deciduous trees testify to their hardiness and relatively low maintenance needs. Both black and white varieties are available. Leaves of the white variety are used to feed silkworms. It's the black fruit that makes for a delicious jam.

♈	**Plant** bareroot in winter
◎	**Harvest** spring, summer
✄	**Prune** annual
❦❦	**Needs cross-pollination** no
♂	**Bears first fruit** second year
☐	**Pot** yes, dwarf variety
☼	**Aspect** sunny position with lots of room for growth
❄	**Frost tolerant** yes
⊥	**Soil pH** 6.6–7.3

Varieties
Red Shahtoot – long purple-red fruit, extended fruiting season, great for jam
Hicks Fancy – small, sweet, dark purple fruit

Nurture
Choose a warm sheltered site with well-drained, fertile soil that has been deeply dug with well-rotted manure or compost. Apply complete fertiliser each winter and mulch with well-rotted manure or compost in spring. Prune to maintain size and remove dead, damaged, diseased or crossed branches as fruit is produced on new growth.

Flavour companions
apricot, basil, blackberry, blueberry, lemon, mint, orange, peach, plum, raspberry

Pectin
low

Ways to preserve
bottled, jam, syrup

How to use
Mix bottled mulberries with apples to make a delicious pie or crumble, or pour syrup over ice cream.

Mulberry jam

Makes about 4 cups

Tradition has it that windfall mulberries are best for eating, but for jam making it's better to pick the fruit before it falls.

1 kg (2 lb 3 oz) mulberries, washed, stalks removed

1 tablespoon powdered pectin

60 ml (¼ cup) freshly squeezed lemon juice

1 kg (2 lb 3 oz) sugar

4 x 250 ml (8½ fl oz) sterilised jars

Place a small saucer in the freezer. Combine the mulberries and pectin in a heavy-based saucepan and warm gently over low heat, crushing the fruit to release the juices. Bring to the boil, add the lemon juice and sugar and stir until the sugar has dissolved, then increase the heat and boil, stirring occasionally, for about 5 minutes.

To test for set, remove the pan from the heat and place a spoonful of jam on the cold saucer. Pop the saucer back in the freezer for a couple of minutes – if the jam wrinkles when pushed, it is ready. If not, cook for another 5 minutes and test again.

When the jam is at setting point, turn off the heat and allow it to sit for 10 minutes. Skim off any foam, then pour the jam into four warm sterilised 250 ml (8½ fl oz) jars (see page 15). Wipe the rims and seal when cold. Store in a cool, dark place and refrigerate after opening.

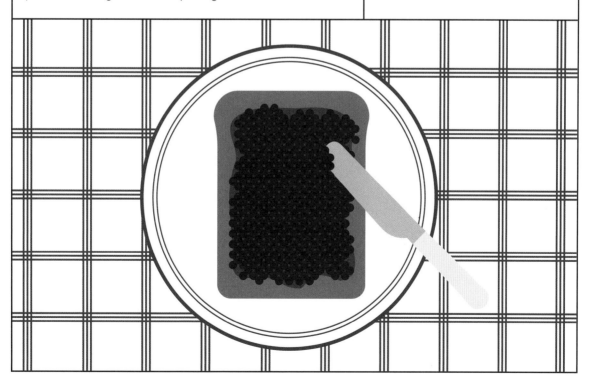

Grapes

If you have a bare arch or pergola in the garden, covering it with grape vines serves two purposes – not only will you have fruit to harvest, but the shade of the green vines offers a delightful outdoor seating area in summer. Pruning vines is an art and depends on how you grow them. Seek expert advice for the first couple of years as plants establish, and it will soon become second nature and a season-marking ritual.

♈	**Plant** bareroot in late autumn, winter; potted in spring
◎	**Harvest** summer, early autumn
✂	**Prune** annual, late winter
❦❦	**Needs cross-pollination** no
♂	**Bears first fruit** third year
⊽	**Pot** yes, with support
☼	**Aspect** warm sunny position with good drainage
❋	**Frost tolerant** yes
⚘	**Soil pH** 6.5–7.0

Grapes

1. Marroo Seedless
2. Menindee Seedless
3. Autumn Royal
4. Golden Muscat

Varieties
Marroo Seedless – large oval fruit with blueish-black skin, firm flesh, seedless
Menindee Seedless –white grape with oval fruit, delicious flavour
Autumn Royal – large purple-black fruit with sweet, firm flesh
Golden Muscat – aromatic fruit with golden yellow skin, slightly muscat-flavoured flesh

Nurture
Plant bareroot vines (see page 192) between late autumn and early spring, potted vines in late spring. Create a support system and place vines 1–1.5 m (3–5 feet) apart. Feed with an all-purpose fertiliser in early spring and summer, applying a high-potash fertiliser in late winter. Mulch with a 5–8 cm (2–3 inch) layer of well-rotted manure or compost, keeping mulch away from the plant stem. Water during dry periods.

Flavour companions
apple, basil, cayenne, cinnamon, coriander, cumin, garlic, ginger, lemon, mint, mustard, paprika, pear, raspberry, star anise, strawberry

Pectin
low

Ways to preserve
bottled, dehydrated, frozen, juice, jelly, jam, chutney, fermented into wine or vinegar

How to use
salads, cheese boards

4.

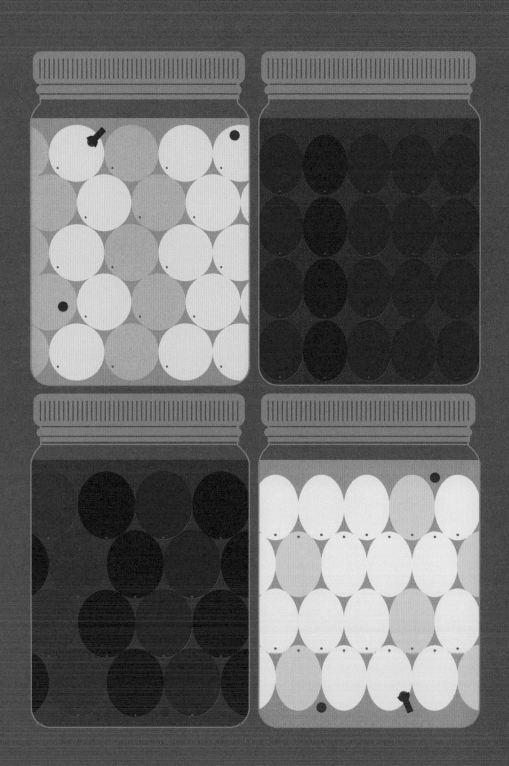

Pickled grapes

Makes about 3½ cups

These sweet/sour grapes are delicious eaten with soft cheese, added to a salad or served with roasted meat. They also make a great addition to a charcuterie platter.

....

Combine the vinegar, sugar, cinnamon, allspice, cloves, peppercorns and 500 ml (1 pint) water in a heavy-based saucepan. Cook, stirring, over low heat until the sugar has dissolved, then increase the heat and bring to the boil.

Pack the grapes into four or five warm sterilised 200 ml (7 fl oz) jars (see page 15), leaving 2.5 cm (1 inch) headspace. Add a small piece of vanilla bean to each jar. Fill the jars with the hot pickling liquid, covering the grapes completely and leaving 1 cm (½ inch) headspace. Wipe the rims, seal the jars and process in a water bath for 15 minutes (see page 14). Leave in a cool, dark place for 4 weeks before using, then refrigerate after opening.

500 ml (1 pint) malt vinegar
400 g (14 oz) sugar
½ cinnamon stick
1 whole allspice
2 whole cloves
5 whole black peppercorns
1 kg (2 lb 3 oz) grapes (green or red), washed, stalks removed
½ vanilla bean, split and cut into 4–5 pieces

4–5 x 200 ml (7 fl oz) sterilised jars

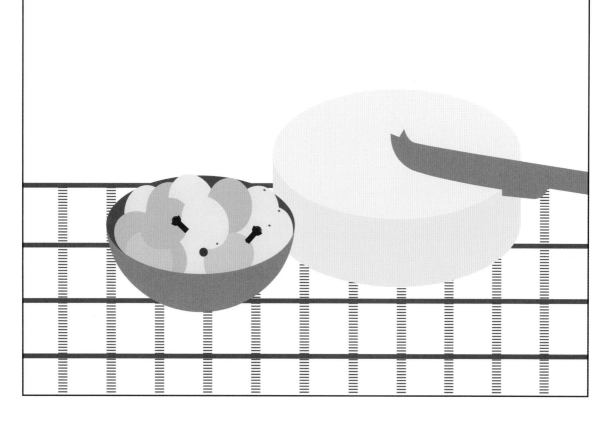

Currants

Ribes rubrum (redcurrant)
Ribes nigrum (blackcurrant)

If you plan on growing currants for preserving, you will need to plant multiple bushes of this sweet and sour berry. The tiny round fruits grow in clusters like grapes and, unless you have numerous bushes, picking enough ripe fruit to make jam or jelly can be challenging. To overcome a slow supply, I pick each bunch as it ripens and place them on a tray to freeze, collecting each day until I have enough for two or three pots of jelly.

Plant bareroot in autumn to early winter

Harvest summer

Prune annual, in winter

Needs cross-pollination not essential

Bears first fruit first to third year

Pot yes

Aspect full sun

Frost tolerant yes

Soil pH 6.0–6.5

1. 2. 3. 4.

Currants

1. Red
2. Golden Currant
3. Pulborough Scarlet
4. Blanca

Varieties

Red – small, compact, upright deciduous shrub with glossy red fruit ready for picking in late summer
Golden Currant – yellow, cream or red flowers with a spicy fragrance with tart yellow to black fruit; leaves turn from green to red in autumn
Pulborough Scarlet – aromatic foliage, reddish-pink flowers, and blue-black fruit
Blanca – small, insignificant flowers produce a translucent ivory fruit in late summer

Nurture

Currants grow best in damp, fertile soil with good drainage where they are sheltered from cold winds. Dig through lots of well-rotted manure or compost before planting 1.5 m (5 feet) apart. Apply general-purpose fertiliser and water well after planting. In spring, fertilise and mulch again with general-purpose fertiliser and a layer of manure or compost around the root zone. Water regularly, especially during dry periods, but avoid water logging. Prune new shoots on one-year-old plants by half, cutting back to an outward facing bud. Remove inward facing buds and shoots to create an open form. Currants fruit on first-year wood. To prune established plants, remove second-year branches, cutting back to an outward facing bud and leaving around ten healthy branches per plant. Remove buds on the inside of branches to maintain an open, airy form.

Flavour companions

aniseed, apple, cherry, lemon, mint, orange, raspberry, strawberry

Pectin

Continues

Blackcurrant and apple jelly

Makes about 1½ cups

This old-fashioned pairing is a classic for a reason. The apples add sweetness and intensify the slightly earthy flavour of blackcurrants.

250 g (9 oz) apples
500 g (1 lb 2 oz) blackcurrants, washed
400 g (14 oz) sugar (approx.)

2 x 200 ml (7 fl oz) sterilised jars

Peel and roughly chop the apples. Place in a heavy-based saucepan with the blackcurrants and 250 ml (1 cup) water, then cover and gently simmer over low heat, stirring occasionally, for 45 minutes.

To strain, pour the mixture into a square of clean muslin sitting in a colander, then gather up the sides and secure with string. Suspend the muslin over a bowl, leaving it to drip overnight. Resist the temptation to squeeze the fruit as this will produce a cloudy jelly.

Place a small saucer in the freezer. Measure the extracted liquid in the bowl and return it to a clean saucepan with 400 g (14 oz) sugar for every 600 ml (1¼ pints) of the liquid. Cook, stirring, over low heat until the sugar has dissolved, then increase the heat and bring to a rolling boil until a set is achieved. To test, remove the pan from the heat and place a spoonful of jelly on the cold saucer. Pop the saucer back in the freezer for a couple of minutes – if the jelly wrinkles when pushed, it is ready. If not, cook for another 5 minutes and test again. When setting point is achieved, skim off any foam, then pour the jelly into two warm sterilised 200 ml (7 fl oz) jars (see page 15). Wipe the rims and seal when cold. Refrigerate after opening.

Redcurrant and raspberry jelly

Makes about 3 cups

This recipe combines two of my favourite red fruits in a perfect balance of tart and sweet. An instant pick-me-up spread on toast, this glistening red jelly may also be used to sandwich biscuits or glaze fruit tarts. Straining the liquid to remove the pips intensifies the glorious colour.

500 g (1 lb 2 oz) redcurrants, washed
500 g (1 lb 2 oz) raspberries, washed
400 g (14 oz) sugar (approx.)

4 x 200 ml (7 fl oz) sterilised jars

Combine the redcurrants, raspberries and 300 ml (10 fl oz) water in a heavy-based saucepan and bring to the boil. Reduce the heat, cover and simmer, stirring occasionally, for 30 minutes or until the fruit has softened.

To strain, pour the mixture into a square of clean muslin sitting in a colander, then gather up the sides and secure with string. Suspend the muslin over a bowl, leaving it to drip overnight. Resist the temptation to squeeze the fruit as this will produce a cloudy jelly.

Place a small saucer in the freezer. Measure the extracted liquid in the bowl and return it to a clean saucepan with 140 g (5 oz) sugar for every 200 ml (7 fl oz) of the liquid. Cook, stirring, over low heat until the sugar has dissolved, then increase the heat and bring to a rolling boil for 5–10 minutes until a set is achieved. To test, remove the pan from the heat and place a spoonful of jelly on the cold saucer. Pop the saucer back in the freezer for a couple of minutes – if the jelly wrinkles when pushed, it is ready. If not, cook for another 5 minutes and test again. When setting point is achieved, skim off any foam, then pour the jelly into four warm sterilised 200 ml (7 fl oz) jars (see page 15). Wipe the rims and seal when cold. Refrigerate after opening.

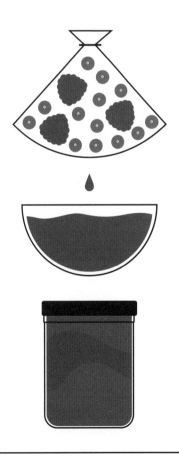

Chapter 04

The preserving garden

Garden basics

Soil

The most critical element of a productive garden is the soil. If this isn't right, plants will struggle from the beginning. Growth will be slow or deformed, plants will produce fewer flowers, and any crop will be disappointing or non-existent. The soil in garden beds needs to be enriched with well-rotted manure and compost before planting. It is possible to buy a potting mix with trace elements required by specific plants, and if you are planning a container garden or a small plot, this can be an easy and quick way to begin. Still, it's important to remember that these mixtures become depleted, and plants will need supplemental food during the growing and flowering seasons.

To grow healthy plants and produce bumper crops, plants need carbon (from the air); hydrogen (from water); oxygen (from water and air); and nitrogen, phosphorus and potassium. Nitrogen aids foliage growth and phosphorus stimulates root growth, so it makes sense that root crops, such as carrots, benefit from a boost of phosphorous, while leafy crops, like cabbage, respond well to the addition of a nitrogen-rich fertiliser. Vegetables grown for their fruit, such as tomatoes, respond to the addition of potassium. No matter what you plant, the growth, vigour and production of a vegetable garden are increased by adding all three basic elements (phosphorous, nitrogen, and potassium). The best way to address this need is by applying well-rotted manure, compost and complete fertiliser.

The aim is to create an open textured soil with air pockets to retain moisture and support the microorganisms that break down organic matter, making minerals and nutrients available to plants.

Soil pH

Growing guides for plants often mention a preference for varying degrees of acidic or alkaline soil. A pH test identifies the state of soil with a pH of 7 (neutral), 14 (highly alkaline) and 0 (highly acidic). The addition of lime, dolomite or chicken manure can reduce acidity. Compost, leaf litter, manure and mulch will reduce alkalinity. A pH of 5.5–7 is a good starting point for most fruit and vegetable gardens. Check pH levels at the beginning of each season and adjust accordingly to give new plants the best possible start.

Soil type

Clay Soil – This heavy, sticky soil will hold its shape if you squeeze it in your hand. Improve poor drainage and a tendency to become compacted with the application of gypsum (follow the instruction on the packet) dug in with compost and well-rotted manure or manure pellets. Finally, add a thick layer of mulch, such as pea straw, and wait a couple of weeks before planting.

Sandy Soil – This light, nutrient-poor soil falls apart when squeezed in your hand. The open structure of sandy soil makes it easy to work with, but quick to dry out. Compost, well-rotted manure or manure pellets add structure and nutrients. A layer of compost helps with moisture retention.

Loamy Soil – The gardener's unicorn, loamy soil, holds its shape but breaks apart when squeezed in your hand. Crops grown in this soil only need species-specific treatment, such as regular watering and fertilising during the growing and flowering seasons.

A note on climate zones

We all have places where we feel most at home, and plants are no different, each has an optimal climate zone – cool summers and frosty winters, warm humid conditions, long summers with weeks and weeks of warm days. It is easy to identify your climate zone, ask at a local nursery or search online for a map to see if you live in a cool, temperate, or tropical zone. Armed with this information it is possible to choose plants, or varieties of plants, that will give the best results in the conditions in your garden. Listings in this book note planting and harvesting times, these timings are also influenced by climate zones. If you live in a cool zone, you may need to sow seeds undercover and plant out later than indicated. Tropical and temperate zones allow for a much longer, sometimes year-round, growing season. Take the time to observe how certain plants grow in your garden, keep a record of the varieties you plant, when you plant, and even the rainfall and temperatures throughout the year. Over time your knowledge, confidence and instinct will grow along with a thriving and productive garden.

Cool: Cold winters, regular frosts, short summers.

Temperate: Four distinct seasons, cool summers, hot winters.

Tropical: Warm winters, high humidity, narrow temperature range.

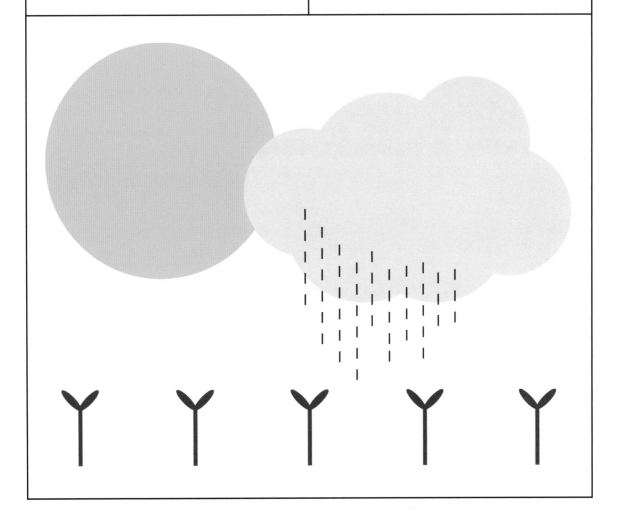

Growing vegetables

Situation

The advice once was that vegetable gardens do best in full sun with the beds running north–south to ensure even sunlight throughout the day. Changing temperatures and days of extreme heat mean this is no longer the case for the summer vegetable garden. The risk of fruit and vegetables cooking on the plant was a rare and notable event but is now part of my planning when creating a new bed or planting a new tree. I look for sites that receive sun in the morning and shade during the hottest part of the day.

Before planting, take some time to watch how the sun moves across the bed or site you plan to plant. Remember the strength and position of the sun changes with the seasons, and this, along with fences, walls and trees, will influence the timing and extent of daily sunlight.

DAILY SUNLIGHT

Full sun: 6 or more hours of direct sunlight.

Partial sun: 4–6 hours of direct sunlight, including some afternoon sun.

Partial shade: 4–6 hours of direct sunlight, most before midday.

Full shade: Fewer than 4 hours of direct sunlight, often described as 'dappled' shade or sunlight.

Compost

Composting can become an obsession; I love the sense of alchemy and knowing I am doing something positive by recycling organic material on-site to create a material essential to improving soil structure and nutrient value. Various methods, contraptions, and systems are available; however, the basics remain the same. A sweet, healthy compost requires a mixture of green (wet) and brown (dry) material, moisture and time. Green matter supplies nitrogen; brown matter supplies carbon. Ideally, you want 60 per cent green material and 40 per cent dry material. Cut any large material into smaller pieces to speed up the decomposition process.

Composting methods are described as 'hot' or 'cold', with hot composting a much faster process than cold. Hot composting, such as the Berkeley method, takes effort and requires sufficient nitrogen to produce a temperature of 50–60°C (120–140°F); this heat accelerates decomposition and kills seeds and pathogens. Materials must be regularly turned or forked over, and moisture levels monitored. Cold composting is a set-and-forget approach and can be very slow, not ideal when you are fired up and ready to plant the new season's vegetable garden.

WHAT TO FEED YOUR COMPOST
Green Matter (Nitrogen)

Grass clippings

Manure (chicken, cow, sheep, horse)

Weeds (without seeds)

Green garden cuttings and leaves

Fruit and vegetable scraps (not citrus, garlic or onions)

Old flowers

Tea leaves and coffee grounds (not teabags)

Fresh leaves

Eggshells

Vegetable oils

Seaweed (rinsed of salt)

Brown Matter (Carbon)

Dried leaves

Pea straw

Sawdust

Newspaper (shredded)

Dried garden cuttings

Manures and fertilisers

Manure adds organic matter to soil improving structure, aeration, and water retention. Fertilisers boost plant health by providing readily available nutrients, minerals, and trace elements. A 'balanced' fertiliser is often all that is needed in the garden. The NPK rating on commercially available fertilisers indicates nitrogen, phosphorous and potassium levels; balanced fertilisers have equal levels of nitrogen, phosphorus and potassium (20–20–20, for example). This rating is a helpful guide to determining if a fertiliser will meet the needs of an individual plant. A higher percentage of nitrogen will encourage foliage development. Potassium contributes to a healthy root system and helps plants set buds, and phosphorus encourages flowers which in turn become fruit.

Manures are described as 'hot' (horse and chicken) or 'cold' (sheep and cow). Chicken manure is a great addition to compost; it accelerates decomposition with high nitrogen and phosphorous levels. 'Fresh' manure should not be applied directly to the garden as it can burn plants. It can take 6–12 months before fresh manure has broken down enough to use in the garden. Waiting for fresh manure to 'rot down' is a slow and often smelly process, but incredibly efficient if you have a ready supply from a chicken coop or stable. The transformation of fresh manure can be accelerated considerably by composting. The Berkeley method produces ready-to-use compost in as little as 3 weeks (details of this process are easy to find online). Bagged manure purchased from

garden suppliers has already broken down and can be applied directly to the garden without further treatment. Pelletised manure can also be applied directly before or after planting. Pelletised or liquid manures are great alternatives if you don't have the time or inclination to use natural manure.

Liquid manure or fertiliser is an excellent way of quickly delivering nutrients to a plant. It is absorbed directly into the roots and foliage, boosting a plant's ability to withstand extreme temperatures. During summer, liquid fertiliser can be applied as often as once a week.

Manure tea is a useful method for adding nutrients to the vegetable garden. Place a spade full of cow or horse manure in an old pillowcase and secure the top with string. Leave the manure to soak in a bucket of water overnight and use the resulting 'tea' to water plants. The manure left in the pillowcase can be added to the compost heap.

Plants will thrive if you supply specific nutrient and mineral needs, prepare soil accordingly, and feed at the appropriate time. A general-purpose liquid fertiliser and slow-release granules are an excellent place to start.

Mulch

Mulch reduces the need for water and suppresses weeds – both time-consuming gardening tasks. Adding this protective layer to the surface of your garden regulates soil temperature and is as important in summer as it is in winter. A thick layer of straw, pea straw, lucerne, or shredded sugarcane can be applied at any time of year, but it is a pre-summer essential.

Germinating seed

Whether you buy, collect your own, or receive them from a gardening friend, seeds offer the easiest and cheapest way to obtain new plants. Specialist seed and plant nurseries can be a great source of rare or heritage seeds; fellow gardeners or community seed-saving banks are also excellent resources. Commercially packaged seed will give details of any specific treatment or approach needed. As a general rule, seeds should be sown in a seed-raising mix, essentially a mixture of fine soil and nutrients. A fine texture allows seeds to be surrounded by soil and offers less resistance to developing roots than a regular potting mix.

You can easily make your own seed-raising mix. The simplest approach is to sieve regular potting mix to remove any large particles, and then add some sifted compost to the soil at a ratio of one part compost to two parts sieved potting mix. Remember to wear a mask when working with finely textured materials that may become airborne.

To adapt the seed-raising mix to individual seeds' requirements – a freer draining mix, for example – begin by blending the following:

1 part vermiculite or sand (for drainage)

2 parts coir (for moisture retention)

½ part aged cow manure (for nutrients)

2 parts fine potting mix

(Adjust individual components according to the seed you are germinating.)

Fill trays or small pots with the potting mix and plant seeds at the recommended depth. Generally, small seeds should be very close to the surface, covered lightly with a fine layer of soil. Use a small, flat-surfaced object such as an old cake tin or piece of wood to gently press seeds into the soil. Keep seeds moist; even a few hours of drying out can kill them off. Water gently, taking care not to disturb the seeds or soil, by using a spray bottle to apply a regular misting of water.

Many seeds benefit from a moist, stable environment. Create a mini greenhouse by placing trays or pots under a small sheet of glass, in a large plastic bag, under an upturned jar, or underneath a clear plastic bottle with the bottom removed.

Planting out

Take care to keep the roots intact when planting seedlings. It can be a struggle to remove commercially purchased seedlings from their flimsy punnets. The least destructive method is to give the punnets a good water before snipping the base off the individual cells and carefully removing each plant. If the root mass is especially matted, you can gently tease it apart at the base to increase the contact between the root and the new soil. Plant seedlings at the recommended depth and spacing, with any necessary support structure in place. Firm the soil, and water with liquid fertiliser before applying a layer of mulch if required.

Crop rotation

Because each plant has specific nutritional needs, growing the same crop in the same place year after year means you will end up planting into soil that is depleted of the elements needed for success. Planning a rotation of crops takes advantage of what the previous crop leaves behind. As a rough guide, vegetable beds should be divided into greens, root crops and legumes and planted in this order. When planning crop rotation, tomatoes can be classed as greens or legumes.

Greens – cabbage, cauliflower, brussels sprouts, tomatoes

Root crops – carrots, beetroot, onions

Legumes – peas, beans, tomatoes

Growing fruit trees

Planting bareroot trees

All gardening is about having faith in the potential of what you plant, but this moves to a new level when I see rows and rows of beds filled with bareroot trees. It takes discipline and a firm shopping list not to go home with twice as many trees as I planned or have space for. Trees in this unencumbered state are also light and easy to move and plant – a considerable influence on any overly ambitious gardener. My experience is that dormant trees seem to get off to a better start, and their leafless form highlights the tree's shape, making it easier to prune branches and impose some shaping at the time of planting.

Bareroot trees should be planted in late winter. If you can't plant them straight away, keep the roots moist by placing them in a temporary hole, or wrapping them in sawdust and hessian, or in thick layers of paper. Water and keep moist until planting out.

Sit trees in a bucket of water and allow them to soak for 2 or 3 hours before planting. Trim any damaged roots with secateurs and cut the branches back to around 40 cm (15 inches) in length, leaving three or four buds on each branch. It sounds like madness and appears to be counter-productive, but this will help the tree recover from the shock of replanting. It is also the first opportunity to set the shape of the tree by removing crossing branches that will crowd the centre of the canopy.

Prepare the soil with the addition of well-rotted manure or compost to the top 15–25 cm (6–10 inches). Fruit trees don't need deeply augmented soil as the roots stay close to the surface to absorb oxygen and nutrients easily. Dig a hole of around 1 m (3 feet) in width and to a depth that sets the tree at the correct level – trees should be planted at the same level as they were in the nursery, and you should be able to see the soil line on the trunk. Insert stakes, if needed, before planting.

Form a small mound at the centre of the hole and position the tree with the roots draped over this mound. Spread the roots to their full extent, untangling any that cross, and making sure they are sloping down. Cover the roots with a layer of soil and gently tamp this down with your feet. Continue to fill the hole, tamping down with each layer.

Build up a small basin around the tree's base in line with the outer edge of the branches and apply a layer of mulch – keeping it away from the trunk. Water-in well, then water again after an hour.

Planting potted fruit trees

When transplanting fruit trees growing in pots, the key to success is to avoid disturbing the roots. Dig a hole with a solid base that is the same depth as the pot and pack the soil firmly around the sides of the root ball. Water-in well, create a basin and apply a layer of mulch as described above.

Pollination

Fruit and nut trees that are described as self-pollinating (or self-fertile) are an excellent choice when you only have room for a single tree. As the name suggests, self-pollinating trees will set fruit without requiring a second tree to provide cross-pollination. Trees that do need a second tree to pollinate and set fruit will often have preferred 'neighbours'; Comice pears, for example, do well when planted with Williams or Beurre Bosc nearby. There was a time when fruit trees growing in backyards were the norm, and it was possible to rely on other trees growing in a nearby garden to provide cross-pollination. I'm not sure this is still a reliable approach. Speak to the experts at the nursery where you purchase your trees to ensure you choose the best variety for your situation.

General maintenance

At a bare minimum, water trees during dry periods and weed regularly to help establish quickly. Mulch to help reduce moisture loss, making sure to keep any mulch away from the tree trunk.

Pruning

Pruning promotes new growth, a healthy tree with good crop production and lets you shape the tree to a manageable size and form. Cutting away branches can be daunting; remember, the aim is to create a framework that makes it easy to access fruit and allows sunlight to the centre of the crown (canopy). The most practical shape is a 'V', with branches low on the trunk so that fruit grows within easy reach and an open crown to admit light and air. Pruning is also the time to remove old, dead or diseased branches and branches that cross or rub against each other. Remove any suckers (new upright growth) sprouting at the tree's base. A good rule is to remove no more than 25 per cent of the tree's crown. If you have an old, neglected fruit tree, it is best to nurse it back to health over several pruning seasons rather than performing an extreme makeover – the shock of removing more than 25 per cent of the crown could be too much for the tree to survive.

Thinning fruit

The sight of branches laden with fruit is enormously satisfying and proof that a tree is healthy, well-positioned and properly nourished. However, it is important to thin a heavily laden tree to ensure the development of full-sized fruit and reduce the risk of damage caused by branches breaking under the weight of their load. Thinning should occur early in the fruiting season. Reduce clusters of fruit growing on established trees to two or three fruits per cluster; the fruit of dwarf or column varieties should be thinned to a single fruit per cluster.

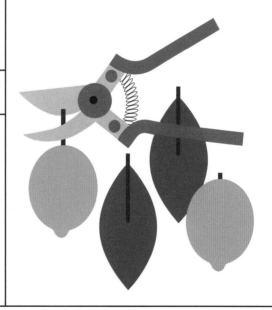

Chapter 05

Preserving charts

Use these preserving charts to plan out your garden, pantry and meals. They include condensed information found throughout this book as well as water bath timing for fruit that is ready to be bottled.

For more information on water baths see page 14. Imperial and cup conversions for liquid measurements are on page 16. Imperial conversions for altitude are on page 15.

FRUIT / VEG / TREE	FLAVOUR COMPANIONS	WAYS TO PRESERVE	HOW TO USE PRESERVES	WATER BATH TIMING (ALTITUDE BELOW 300 M)
CUCUMBER	chives, coriander, cumin, dill, garlic, lemon, mint, olive, paprika, parsley, spring onion, strawberry, tomato	pickled	salads, sandwiches, burgers, sauce ravigote, potato salads	N/A
ZUCCHINI	basil, capers, coriander, garlic, lemon, mint, oregano, parsley, tomato, walnut	pickled, relish	sandwiches, cheese boards, antipasto, salads	N/A
TOMATOES	basil, capsicum, chilli, chives, cucumber, garlic, ginger, onion, oregano	bottled, chutney, paste, puree, relish, sauce	pastas, stews, soups, cheese boards, with grilled meat	Add ¼ teaspoon of citric acid for every 500 ml of tomatoes **CRUSHED – Hot pack** 250–500 ml, 35 minutes 750 ml–1 litre, 45 minutes **Altitude adjustment** 301–900 m + 5 minutes 900–1830 m + 10 minutes above 1830 m + 15 minutes **SAUCE – Hot pack** 250–500 ml, 35 minutes 750 ml–1 litre, 40 minutes **Altitude adjustment** 301–900 m + 5 minutes 900–1830 m + 10 minutes above 1830 m + 15 minutes **WHOLE OR HALVED, WITH WATER – Hot and raw pack** 250–500 ml, 40 minutes 750 ml–1 litre, 45 minutes **WITHOUT WATER – Raw pack** 250 ml–1 litre, 85 minutes **Altitude adjustment** 301–900 m + 5 minutes 900–1830 m + 10 minutes above 1830 m + 15 minutes
CAPSICUMS	capers, eggplant, garlic, green beans, lemon, olive, onion, tomato	pickled, sauce, roasted and preserved in oil	antipasto, pizza, salads, stews	N/A
CHILLIES	coriander, cumin, garlic, ginger, lime, tomato	jam, jelly, pickled, dried	cheese boards, sandwiches, stews, salads	N/A
CAPERS	basil, chilli, citrus, dill, eggplant, green beans, parsley	brined, salted	potato or green bean salads, chicken dishes, fish dishes (especially salmon)	N/A
GARLIC	basil, capsicum, fennel, parsley, potato, tomato	dried, butter, frozen, paste	stews, sauces, marinades, for basting meats	N/A
GINGER	basil, beans, chilli, coriander, cumin, garlic, lemon, lime, mint, orange, rhubarb, turmeric	candied, dried, cordial, in sherry	dried – soups, stews; candied – baking; preserved in sherry – in stir-fry	N/A

FRUIT / VEG / TREE	FLAVOUR COMPANIONS	WAYS TO PRESERVE	HOW TO USE PRESERVES	WATER BATH TIMING (ALTITUDE BELOW 300 M)
BEETROOT	almond, allspice, apple, basil, blueberry, caraway seed, carrot, cinnamon, coriander, cucumber, cumin, dill, fennel, garlic, lemon, mint, orange, paprika, parsley, pepper, tarragon, thyme, walnut	pickled	salads, burgers, charcuterie	**SLICED – Hot pack** 250 ml–1 litre, 30 minutes **Altitude adjustment** 301–900 m + 5 minutes 900–1830 m + 10 minutes above 1830 m + 15 minutes
CARROTS	caraway seed, celery, coriander seed, dill, fennel, garlic, ginger, mustard, nutmeg, parsley, pepper	jam, pickled, puree	salads, sandwiches, charcuterie, cheese boards, as a tasty side dish	N/A
FENNEL	capers, capsicum, chilli, garlic, lemon, olive, orange, tomato, walnut	pickled	salads, served with fish or braised meats	N/A
CABBAGE	apple, beetroot, caraway seed, carrot, celery, coriander seed, dill, fennel, garlic, ginger, mustard, nutmeg, onion, orange, parsley, potato, sour cherry	pickled	in pork dishes, salads, with baked potatoes, scrambled eggs, avocado toast	N/A
BEANS	almond, beetroot, capers, capsicum, celery, chilli, chives, coriander, cumin, garlic, lemon, mint, olive, parsley, pine nut, spring onion, tarragon, tomato	pickled, dried, frozen	salads, sandwiches, charcuterie, antipasto	N/A
CORN	butter, capsicum, chilli, coriander, cumin, lime, tomato	relish, chutney, pickled	burgers, salads, antipasto, cheese boards, baked potatoes	N/A
RHUBARB	cinnamon, orange, rosewater, strawberry, vanilla	relish, jam, cordial, candied, syrup	cheese boards, cake filling, to glaze sweet or savoury dishes; syrup mixed with drinks	N/A
MINT	basil, beans, carrot, clove, cucumber, cumin, dill, ginger, lemon, oregano, parsley, potato, thyme, tomato	jelly, vinegar, butter	on grilled or roast lamb	N/A
BASIL	balsamic vinegar, beans, carrot, clove, garlic, lemon, lime, mint, peach, strawberry, tomato, zucchini	puree, frozen	soups, stews, pizza, pastas	N/A
TARRAGON	asparagus, basil, broad beans, carrot, chicken, dill, mint, parsley, thyme, tomato, zucchini	frozen, butter, dried	sauces, garnish, with fish dishes, on roasted vegetables	N/A

FRUIT / VEG / TREE	FLAVOUR COMPANIONS	WAYS TO PRESERVE	HOW TO USE PRESERVES	WATER BATH TIMING (ALTITUDE BELOW 300 M)
APPLES	allspice, apricot, blackberry, cardamom, cherry, cinnamon, clove, cumin, currant, date, ginger, nutmeg, orange, pears, plum, quince, star anise, vanilla	bottled, jelly, sauce	apple sauce with roast pork, bottled pie filling, desserts; jelly used to glaze sweet and savoury dishes	**SLICED – Hot pack** 750 ml–1 litre, 20 minutes **Altitude adjustment** 301–900 m + 5 minutes 900–1830 m + 10 minutes above 1830 m + 15 minutes
CRABAPPLES	allspice, blackberry, cardamom, cinnamon, clove, coriander, cumin, ginger, nutmeg, pear, plum, quince, star anise, vanilla	jam, jelly, pickled	to glaze sweet or savoury dishes; spiced pickled crabapples with roast pork	**SLICED – Hot pack** 250–500 ml, 20 minutes **Altitude adjustment** 301–900 m + 5 minutes 900–1830 m + 10 minutes above 1830 m + 15 minutes
PEARS	allspice, apple, apricot, basil, blackberry, blueberry, cardamom, cherry, chocolate, cinnamon, clove, date, ginger, lemon, mace, mint, nutmeg, orange, passionfruit, quince, raspberry, rhubarb, star anise, strawberry, vanilla, walnut	butter, bottled, chutney	spread on a crumpet; in pies, cakes and crumbles; mixed through yoghurt	**HALVED – Hot pack** 250–500 ml, 20 minutes 750 ml–1 litre, 25 minutes **Altitude adjustment** 301–900 m + 5 minutes 900–1830 m + 10 minutes above 1830 m + 15 minutes
QUINCE	allspice, apple, cinnamon, clove, ginger, honey, lemon, orange, vanilla	jam, jelly, paste, chutney	cheese boards	Quince can be bottled after they have been poached or slow roasted **SLICED – Hot pack** 250–500 ml, 15 minutes **Altitude adjustment** 301–900 m + 5 minutes 900–1830 m + 10 minutes above 1830 m + 15 minutes
ORANGES	apple, apricot, basil, blackberry, blueberry, cardamom, cherry, cinnamon, clove, coriander, cumin, cumquat, date, fennel, fig, ginger, grape, grapefruit, lemon, lime, mint, nutmeg, paprika, parsley, passionfruit, peach, pear, plum, quince, raspberry, rhubarb, saffron, star anise, strawberry, thyme, tomato, walnut	marmalade, jelly, cordial, dried, syrup	cakes, puddings, salads	N/A
GRAPEFRUIT	basil, ginger, lemon, lime, mint, orange, raspberry, rosemary, star anise, strawberry, tarragon, thyme	marmalade, jelly, cordial, dried, dehydrated	glaze for sweet and savoury dishes, in steamed pudding, paired with soft cheeses	N/A
LEMONS	apple, apricot, basil, bay leaf, blackberry, blueberry, cardamom, cayenne, cherry, cinnamon, date, ginger, gooseberry, grape, grapefruit, lime, mint, orange, oregano, parsley, passionfruit, peach, pear, plum, poppy seed, quince, raspberry, rhubarb, sage, thyme, vanilla	marmalade, cordial, candied, frozen, cured in jars, paste, butter, pickled, dried	salsas, chimichurri, salads, stews, marinades, pastas, desserts, vinaigrette, with roasted vegetables, on fish	N/A

FRUIT / VEG / TREE	FLAVOUR COMPANIONS	WAYS TO PRESERVE	HOW TO USE PRESERVES	WATER BATH TIMING (ALTITUDE BELOW 300 M)
LIMES	apple, apricot, coconut, coriander, ginger, gooseberry, grapefruit, lemon, mint, orange, passionfruit, plum, raspberry, strawberry, tomato	marmalade, cordial, candied, frozen, dehydrated, dried, fermented, paste, butter	baking, vinaigrettes, marinades, mixed through Greek yoghurt, in margaritas	N/A
APRICOTS	apple, blackberry, blueberry, cardamom, cherry, cinnamon, ginger, lemon, nutmeg, orange, peach, plum, raspberry, saffron, strawberry, vanilla	chutney, jam, bottled, dried	chutney in coleslaw dressing; jam, warmed to glaze fruit tarts; cakes, cobblers, crumbles	**HALVED OR SLICED – Hot pack** 250–500 ml, 20 minutes 750 ml–1 litre, 25 minutes **Raw pack** 250–500 ml, 25 minutes 750 ml–1 litre, 30 minutes **Altitude adjustment** 301–900 m + 5 minutes 900–1830 m + 10 minutes above 1830 m + 15 minutes
PEACHES	allspice, almond, apple, apricot, basil, bay leaf, blackberry, blueberry, cherry, cinnamon, clove, ginger, lemon, lime, mace, mint, nutmeg, orange, passionfruit, pineapple, plum, raspberry, saffron, star anise, strawberry, tarragon, vanilla	bottled, jam, chutney, dried	salsa, topped with crumble and baked for a quick dessert, sliced on top of yoghurt and granola, or added to a salad	**HALVED OR SLICED – Hot pack** 250–500 ml, 15 minutes 750 ml–1 litre, 20 minutes **Raw pack** 250–500 ml, 25 minutes 750 ml–1 litre, 30 minutes **Altitude adjustment** 301–900 m + 5 minutes 900–1830 m + 10 minutes above 1830 m + 15 minutes
PLUMS	allspice, almond, apricot, bay leaf, cherry, cinnamon, clove, coriander, ginger, lemon, mace, nectarine, nutmeg, orange, peach, raspberry, star anise, strawberry, vanilla	jam, sauce, chutney, bottled, frozen	marinades, as a glaze, in cakes and puddings, paired with a soft goat's cheese	**HALVED OR WHOLE – Hot and raw pack** 250–500 ml, 20 minutes 750 ml–1 litre, 25 minutes **Altitude adjustment** 301–900 m + 5 minutes 900–1830 m + 10 minutes above 1830 m + 15 minutes
CHERRIES	allspice, apricot, cinnamon, clove, coconut, ginger, lemon, nectarine, orange, peach, plum, quince, raspberry, vanilla	bottled, dried, pickled, jam, syrup, frozen	dried cherries in muffins; frozen cherries with cream; in pies, over ice cream	**WHOLE, SWEET OR SOUR – Hot pack** 250–500 ml, 15 minutes 750 ml–1 litre, 20 minutes **Raw pack** 250 ml–1 litre, 25 minutes **Altitude adjustment** 301–900 m + 5 minutes 900–1830 m + 10 minutes above 1830 m + 15 minutes
FIGS	apple, blackberry, cardamom, cinnamon, fennel seed, ginger, grape, honey, lemon, orange, orange, peach, pear, raspberry, rosemary	bottled, candied, jam, dried, syrup, frozen, chutney	cakes, pies, tarts, salads, cheese boards, pizza, in stuffing	**WHOLE – Hot pack, must be acidified** 250–500 ml, 45 minutes 750 ml–1 litre, 50 minutes **Altitude adjustment** 301–900 m + 5 minutes 900–1830 m + 10 minutes above 1830 m + 15 minutes
OLIVES	chilli, coriander, cumin, fennel, garlic, lemon, onion, orange, oregano, parsley, pepper, thyme, tomato	pickled, dried, paste	dried olives chopped and sprinkled on pasta, pizza and salads; olive paste on cheese boards and bread	N/A

FRUIT / VEG / TREE	FLAVOUR COMPANIONS	WAYS TO PRESERVE	HOW TO USE PRESERVES	WATER BATH TIMING (ALTITUDE BELOW 300 M)
WALNUT	apple, chocolate, cinnamon, fig, nutmeg, orange, peach, pear, plum, vanilla	candied, pickled (green), frozen	cheese boards, syrup, added to beef stew, in desserts	N/A
ALMOND	apple, apricot, blackberry, blackcurrant, blueberry, cardamom, cherry, cinnamon, fig, garlic, ginger, grape, nectarine, olive, peach, pear, raspberry, rhubarb, strawberry	butter, candied, frozen, pickled (green)	baking	N/A
PASSIONFRUIT	coriander, ginger, lemon, lime, mango, orange, peach, pear, pineapple, strawberry, vanilla	frozen (whole, or separate pulp and place in ice cube trays), jam, bottled, dehydrated	baking, desserts	**Cold pack** Place in warm water bath, bring to the boil and process for 15 minutes
RASPBERRIES	citrus, ginger, mint, redcurrant, rhubarb, strawberry, thyme, vanilla	vinegar, frozen, dehydrated, jam, jelly	salad dressing, vinaigrette, on pancakes, diluted in soda water, baking, desserts	**WHOLE – Hot pack** 250 ml–1 litre, 15 minutes **Altitude adjustment** 301–900 m + 5 minutes 900–1830 m + 5 minutes above 1830 m + 10 minutes **Raw pack** 250–500 ml, 15 minutes **Altitude adjustment** 301–900 m + 5 minutes 900–1830 m + 5 minutes above 1830 m + 10 minutes 750 ml–1 litre, 20 minutes **Altitude adjustment** 301–900 m + 5 minutes 900–1830 m + 10 minutes above 1830 m + 15 minutes
BLACKBERRIES	apple, apricot, blueberry, cinnamon, clove, ginger, lemon, mint, mulberry, orange, peach, pear, raspberry, strawberry, vanilla	bottled, dehydrated (whole, chopped or powdered), jam, frozen	baking, desserts, pie filling	See Raspberries
BLUEBERRIES	fig, ginger, honey, lemon, lime, nutmeg, orange, peach, vanilla	jam, jelly, dehydrated (whole, chopped or powdered), frozen, sauce, syrup	baking, desserts	See Raspberries
STRAWBERRIES	apple, apricot, balsamic vinegar, basil, blackberry, blueberry, boysenberry, cardamom, cinnamon, clove, coriander, cumquat, ginger, gooseberry, grape, grapefruit, lemon, lime, mint, nutmeg, orange, passionfruit, peach, pineapple, plum, pomegranate, raspberry, rhubarb, vanilla	jam, jelly, dehydrated (whole, chopped or powdered), frozen, sauce, syrup	baking, desserts	See Raspberries
GOOSEBERRIES	apple, bay leaf, coriander, lemon, mint, mustard, orange, strawberry, vanilla	chutney, jelly, jam, frozen (whole or pureed)	with cheese or oily fish; jam, on toast and muffins; spooned on top of ice cream	See Raspberries

FRUIT / VEG / TREE	FLAVOUR COMPANIONS	WAYS TO PRESERVE	HOW TO USE PRESERVES	WATER BATH TIMING (ALTITUDE BELOW 300 M)
MULBERRIES	apricot, basil, blackberry, blueberry, lemon, mint, orange, peach, plum, raspberry	bottled, jam, syrup	mix bottled mulberries with apples to make a delicious pie or crumble; pour syrup over ice cream	**WHOLE – Hot pack** 250 ml–1 litre, 15 minutes **Altitude adjustment** 301–900 m + 5 minutes 900–1830 m + 5 minutes above 1830 m + 10 minutes **Raw pack** 250–500 ml, 15 minutes **Altitude adjustment** 301–900 m + 5 minutes 900–1830 m + 5 minutes above 1830 m + 10 minutes 750 ml–1 litre, 20 minutes **Altitude adjustment** 301–900 m + 5 minutes 900–1830 m + 10 minutes above 1830 m + 15 minutes
GRAPES	apple, basil, cayenne, cinnamon, coriander, cumin, garlic, ginger, lemon, mint, mustard, paprika, pear, raspberry, star anise, strawberry	bottled, dehydrated, frozen, juice, jelly, jam, chutney, fermented into wine or vinegar	salads, cheese boards	**WHOLE – Hot pack** 250 ml–1 litre, 10 minutes **Altitude adjustment** 301–900 m + 5 minutes 900–1830 m + 5 minutes above 1830 m + 10 minutes **Raw pack** 250–500 ml, 15 minutes **Altitude adjustment** 301–900 m + 5 minutes 900–1830 m + 5 minutes above 1830 m + 10 minutes 750 ml–1 litre, 20 minutes **Altitude adjustment** 301–900 m + 5 minutes 900–1830 m + 10 minutes above 1830 m + 15 minutes
CURRANTS	aniseed, apple, cherry, lemon, mint, orange, raspberry, strawberry	jam, jelly, frozen, dehydrated	High pectin makes currants a great addition to fruit with low-setting qualities such as berries. Use redcurrant jelly to make Cumberland sauce, glaze a rack of lamb, add a glistening finish to fruit tarts or a jewel-like centre to thumbprint biscuits.	**WHOLE – Hot pack** 250 ml–1 litre, 15 minutes **Altitude adjustment** 301–900 m + 5 minutes 900–1830 m + 5 minutes above 1830 m + 10 minutes **Raw pack** 250–500 ml, 15 minutes **Altitude adjustment** 301–900 m + 5 minutes 900–1830 m + 5 minutes above 1830 m + 10 minutes 750 ml–1 litre, 20 minutes **Altitude adjustment** 301–900 m + 5 minutes 900–1830 m + 10 minutes above 1830 m + 15 minutes

Index

Note: **Bolded** entries indicate plants that have individual profiles within the book.

Notes

First published in Australia in 2023
by Thames & Hudson Australia Pty Ltd
11 Central Boulevard, Portside Business Park
Port Melbourne, Victoria 3207
ABN: 72 004 751 964

First published in the United Kingdom in 2023
By Thames & Hudson Ltd
181a High Holborn
London WC1V 7QX

First published in the United States of America in 2023
By Thames & Hudson Inc.
500 Fifth Avenue
New York, New York 10110

The Preserving Garden © Thames & Hudson Australia 2023

Text © Jo Turner 2023
Illustrations © Ashlea O'Neill 2023

26 25 24 23   5 4 3 2 1

The moral right of the author has been asserted.

Thames & Hudson Australia wishes to acknowledge that
Aboriginal and Torres Strait Islander people are the first
storytellers of this nation and the traditional custodians of
the land on which we live and work. We acknowledge their
continuing culture and pay respect to Elders past, present
and future.

ISBN 978-1-760-76286-5

ISBN 978-1-760-76382-4 (U.S. edition)

A catalogue record for this
book is available from the
National Library of Australia

British Library Cataloguing-in-Publication Data
A catalogue record for this book is available from the
British Library

Library of Congress Control Number 2023933714

Every effort has been made to trace accurate ownership of
copyrighted text and visual materials used in this book. Errors
or omissions will be corrected in subsequent editions, provided
notification is sent to the publisher.

Design: Ashlea O'Neill | Salt Camp Studio
Series concept: Jo Turner
Editing: Rachel Carter & Shannon Grey
Printed and bound in China by C&C Offset Printing Co., Ltd

FSC® is dedicated to the promotion of responsible forest
management worldwide. This book is made of material from
FSC®-certified forests and other controlled sources.

Be the first to know about our new releases,
exclusive content and author events by visiting
thamesandhudson.com.au
thamesandhudson.com
thamesandhudsonusa.com

ACKNOWLEDGEMENTS

The love I have for gardening and preserving comes from Mum,
and I still rely on her wisdom. I called on her countless times
while writing this book, thanks Mum. The idea for *The Preserving
Garden* emerged from one of the many and wide-ranging
conversations I had with Kirsten Abbott; her publishing skill,
insight and style are beyond compare, and talking books and
ideas with her is one of my favourite pastimes. Early work on
the book was carefully guided by Kirsten and Lisa Schuurman.
Skilful text wrangling was managed with care by Shannon Grey
and Rachel Carter, their editorial finesse transformed my unruly
text. Ashlea O'Neill's illustrations are a revelation and a joy,
a playful and accurate rendering of the visual delights of both
the garden and preserves.